D0821456

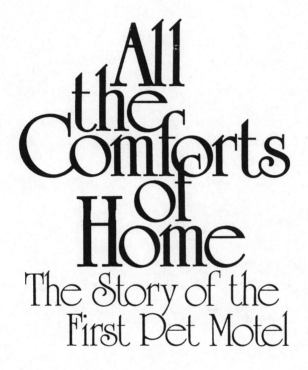

# All the Comforts of Home

## The Story of the First Pet Motel

*Robert X. Leeds*

**DODD, MEAD & COMPANY**
NEW YORK

Published by Dodd, Mead & Company, Inc.
71 Fifth Avenue, New York, N. Y. 10003
Distributed in Canada by
McClelland and Stewart Limited, Toronto
Manufactured in the United States of America
First Edition

1  2  3  4  5  6  7  8  9  10

**Library of Congress Cataloging-in-Publication Data**
Leeds, Robert X.
  All the comforts of home.

  Includes index.
  1. Pet boarding facilities.  I. Title.
SF414.3.L43  1987      636.08'3      87-610
ISBN 0-396-08881-3

# DEDICATION

*". . . Dreams are highways of the heart . . .
    You make a wish and the journey starts."*

To my wife, Peggy . . . My traveling companion.

To my children, Michael, Leslie, Gail, and Myong Ok, whose support and confidence sustained us on our pilgrimage.

*". . . When a cause is just, just men will rise to the cause."*

A special expression of gratitude to my son, Marc, who arose to the cause. We were never alone in our travail.

And to all those men and women of the pet-care industry who share in a noble quest for our companion animals.

# CONTENTS

INTRODUCTION                                           xiii

Chapter 1
  IN THE BEGINNING                                        1

Chapter 2
  THE LESSON OF SOCRATES                                 11

Chapter 3
  PET BOARDING IN AMERICA                                18

Chapter 4
  THE PERFECT PET CARE FACILITY                          26

Chapter 5
  THE QUEST FOR FINANCING                                42

Chapter 6
  CHICAGO, THE PROMISING LAND                            47

Chapter 7
  AN OFFER I COULDN'T REFUSE                             54

Chapter 8
  IT'S ONLY MONEY                                        61

Chapter 9
  THE GUESTS ARRIVE                                      67

Chapter 10
  EMPLOYEES ARE SPECIAL PEOPLE                           76

Chapter 11
  ROOM SERVICE, PLEASE!                                  84

Chapter 12
  McDOLLAR'S, THEY'LL HAVE IT THEIR
  WAY . . . OR ELSE                                      92

Chapter 13
SPECIAL GUESTS—SPECIAL PROBLEMS                98

Chapter 14
THE WANTED AND THE WANTING                    107

Chapter 15
VIRUS STRIKES THE CATTERY                     119

Chapter 16
DOGGED BY VETERINARY VENGEANCE                129

Chapter 17
GROOMING FOR HEALTH                           139

Chapter 18
THE GERIATRIC TRADE                           147

Chapter 19
SOMEDAY YOUR "PRINCE" WILL COME               157

Chapter 20
A DREAM IS SHATTERED                          165

Chapter 21
THE DECISION IS MADE                          172

Chapter 22
AGAIN . . . AGAIN . . . AND AGAIN             178

Appendix
SELECTING A BOARDING FACILITY                 185

INDEX                                         191

# ACKNOWLEDGMENTS

I cannot believe that any accomplishment is without the benefit of many unseen and unheralded collaborators. Certainly ours was not. Though there were many who made our struggle easier, I would be remiss if I didn't pay special tribute to the following Doctors of Veterinary Medicine.

Robert W. Abell, Warren Anderson, J. W. Barnes, Alvin M. Becker, Leland Carmichael, Fred S. David, Lynn Doner, David I. Epstein, Robert F. Going, Roger A. Halvorsen, Ralph O. Holstein, Debbie J. Hasse, Jan Hasse, James E. Kurzydlo, Theodore J. Lafeber, Robert Mahr, A. Thomas Maiolo, Douglas McGregor, Imre Pagi, Roy V. H. Pollock, Robert G. Schirmer, Lewis Seidenberg, Erwin Small, Ralph S. Wilhelm, Thompson T. Wright, and Phillip Zand.

I also wish to express our appreciation to the entire staff of the following veterinary clinics and hospitals: A-Northwest Emergency Veterinary Center, Abell Animal Hospital, Ace Animal Hospital, Barnes Bone Animal Hospital, Bayshore Animal Hospital, Berwyn Veterinary Association, Blum Animal Hospital, Bone Animal Hospital, Care Animal Hospital of Arlington Heights, Countryside Animal Clinic, Forest Lakes Animal Clinic, McCormick Animal Hospital, Misner-Holley Animal Hospital, Niles Animal Hospital, Rand Road Animal Hospital, Riser Animal Hospital, Rohlwing Road Animal Hospital, Terry Animal Hospital, Wauconda Animal Clinic, Wheaton Animal Hospital, and Wilhelm Veterinary Clinic.

I wish also to express my gratitude to the Oil Dri

Corporation, Quaker Oats Company, Ralston Purina Company, Simonson Mills Company, Suburban Surgical Company, and the Wayne Feed Company for their assistance in the development of our facilities and programs.

I must also acknowledge a debt of gratitude to all the men and women who, as employees, have shared and been a part of this experience.

Undoubtedly there are numerous other veterinarians, manufacturers, and laymen who deserve to share in these acknowledgments and who I have neglected to mention. I sincerely apologize for the oversight.

Six people deserve singular recognition for having made possible the happy ending to this chronicle: Ralph Brown and Robert O. Case of Walsh, Case, Coale & Brown; David R. Bromwell, D.V.M., Director, Illinois Dept. of Agriculture; Dr. Jim Corbin, Professor of Animal Science, University of Illinois; and not the least, Greg Getschman and Jane Jordan Browne of Multimedia Product Development, Inc., my literary mentors.

*And God created the heavens and the Earth and on the evening of the sixth day brought forth all the animals that would dwell thereon: and it was good . . . and God saw that it was good. Then, He said, 'I shall create mankind and give it dominion o'er all the Earth and the animals that dwell thereon that he shall reign with understanding and with compassion. But, God was very tired, so He appointed a committee. . . . Alas!*

Rexel

# INTRODUCTION

My wife Peggy answered the telephone, and a serious voice on the other end of the line inquired, "I'd like to reserve a room for a camel. Do you have one?"

"Yes, we do," she cheerfully replied. "We can board anything that walks, creeps, crawls, hops, swims, flies, or slithers, as long as it's not vicious or poisonous."

"Oh, good," the caller sighed. "There is one thing, though. Bernice is pregnant."

"We have a maternity service," Peggy responded.

"Well, Bernice is very special to us and we want to be sure she gets good care. I understand you have wall-to-wall carpeting with brass beds, Sealy mattresses, and Snoopy sheets. Will she also have these?"

Peggy paused briefly and then explained that such furnishings were only available in the Imperial and Regency Suites for dogs. A camel would have to settle for something less—a bed of straw in the stable or barn.

After several minutes more of discussion, the caller identified himself as Wally Phillips, a well-known Chicago talk-show host. A recording of the conversation was played for his audience for the next week.

For Peggy and me, the call was not at all unusual. We run a million-dollar motel for animals just outside of Chicago, in Prairie View, Illinois, and the amenities she had just described were but a few that we offer to our animal guests. For thirteen years, we have catered to that unique and specially privileged member of the American household—the family pet.

To deny that we were directed to this vocation by some unseen hand of fate would be to ignore the substance of providence. What reason would support forsaking a secure and comfortable middle age to embark on such a dubious quest as bringing reform to the pet-boarding industry?

It was not logic that directed us to this interest. Instead, like thousands of pet owners, our concern was inflamed by the tragic and needless loss of our own pet in a boarding kennel. Unlike many pet owners, however, we did not choose to forget the incident, nor did we want to forgive the prevailing system that encouraged it. We wanted a change in the way pets are cared for.

Our entry into the pet-boarding industry was not without incident, and it is true that there were times when exasperation or exhaustion tempted us to flee.

Yet, whenever these doubts arose, we had only to hear the joyful yapping of a departing four-legged guest, or the shrill chatter of voices issuing from the variety of brightly plumed birds in the aviary, to reassure us. The quest was worthwhile, the goal worth striving for.

The heartfelt pleasures derived from working with animals and with the hundreds of other kennel owners who shared our concerns more than mitigated the occasional adversity. In the end, our labors forged an example that would not tarnish before the acid recriminations of those intent on perpetuating an unprincipled industry.

Some detractors may still claim that American Pet Motels is nothing more than a glorified kennel, but it is a fact that we have boarded more than twelve thousand dogs, cats, birds, and miscellaneous animals each year and we have done it without any of the problems our peers predicted.

While America's largest kennels boasted when they grossed $100,000 a year, we soon took in almost that amount in a single month. But it is not the quantity of pets served or the amount of dollars received in which we take our greatest pride. Our outstanding achievement is the virtual elimination of any illnesses, injuries, or deaths to the pets while in our care. From the beginning, we said it could be done. It had been our sole objective, and it remains our most prized accomplishment. We conceived a radically different concept for the public boarding of people's pets, and we brought that concept into being with an unbelievable degree of success.

I admit our entry into the pet-boarding business was an act of arrogant brashness. Neither Peggy nor I had any training or experience in this field. To compound the ridiculous, we wanted to build a $250,000 pet motel that would not only board dogs and cats, but any type of animal that a person would call a pet.

In revealing our plans to our closest friends and the family veterinarian, we refuted every conceivable argument with the same impenetrable self-assuredness. This was due to something deep inside us, something that refused to let us accept that collies couldn't be boarded because "they would just pine away," or that it was natural that some pets always died from loneliness, or "grievance disease," as our veterinarian called it.

Nor could we accept that it was normal for someone's pet to run away from a shelter or to become injured or maimed while being boarded there. Perhaps what disturbed us most was the passive attitude of veterinarians and kennel operators toward these conditions.

With very few exceptions, those in the industry maintained that conditions could not be changed. Instinctively, we were just as sure that a facility could be built and operated that would eliminate all the evils associated with kenneling an animal. It was our dream to build such a facility. To dispel any doubts about our intentions, we would also inaugurate two changes that were unheard of in the pet-boarding industry. Our boarding contract would specifically accept liability for every pet. In addition, we would give each pet owner a written guarantee that his pet would go home in as good, or better, condition than when it came in, or we would reimburse the owner up to two hundred and fifty dollars to return the pet to its original condition. To those in the business, it was insanity. To us, it was a challenge. We knew it could be done. We knew we could do it.

# IN THE BEGINNING

As I sat across from my boss's desk one bleak December day in 1970 and told him what I planned to do, he obviously must have questioned my sanity.

I had had a few odd pets in my lifetime, but I was an engineer, not a zoo keeper. I had started at General Motors seventeen years before as a clerk and now had attained a position and privileges most employees would have been eternally grateful for.

In addition to a very generous salary, I was receiving an annual bonus and shares of stock in the company. I was able to select five new company cars each year, changing them as soon as the odometer reached three thousand miles. For the first time in a lifetime of insecurity and frequent periods of unemployment, I was secure.

All the advantages of working for General Motors were reviewed for me by my manager. At forty-three years of age, there was still opportunity to garner an even larger share of the good life.

After all, he reasoned, I hadn't started with the company until I was twenty-six. Over the past years, I had not only proved my ability as an industrial engineer, but I had worked equally hard during my "free" time, acquiring first a bachelor's degree and then a master's degree from Wayne State University. Because I had quit high school to enlist during World War II, I began my college studies without even an eleventh-grade education, but I concluded my master's program with the Sigma Iota Epsilon scholarship key.

I had been chosen to serve as a consultant with the corporation's manufacturing staff and on several occasions was sent to the General Motors Institute for advanced courses in engineering and financial and managerial techniques. The company had invested in my education and we had both benefited. My record also listed almost a dozen special assignments for which I had been selected.

"Are you really going to give all of this up to run a dog kennel?" my manager asked incredulously.

"Not a dog kennel," I corrected him politely. "A motel. A pet motel."

He kept his eyes focused on mine as he refolded my letter of resignation and placed it back in its original envelope. He held it out to me.

"Why don't you take it back and think about it for a few days." Almost confidentially, he said, "I won't mention it to anybody. Think it over." His head was nodding up and down as if he was giving his consent.

"No," I replied, smiling. My stomach was churning inside and there was a strong temptation to take the letter back, but inside I knew I mustn't weaken. This newly awakened concern for animal welfare and the forces that had compelled me to make a commitment were stronger than any logical persuasions. I could procrastinate no longer.

I stood up awkwardly, almost falling over the chair, as I tried to move out of reach of the envelope. I had given my official notice. I was saying good-bye to all my unearned shares in the stock bonus program, my pension plan, and the alluring benefits one struggles a lifetime to achieve, and I was turning it all in for a dream.

When I drove my freshly washed car out of the company garage that night in December 1970, my feeling was one of exhilaration. It had to be the kind of feeling experienced by someone who learns he's won a lottery or some other long sought-after prize.

If I had even the remotest suspicion of certain future events, I might have gone right back to the office to claim that letter. For some, it is a fine line that separates a dream from an obsession. For me, there was no difference.

During almost all of my childhood, my family had always had some kind of mutt as a household pet. I never really conceived of a family as being complete without a dog or cat to share the daily experience of family life. When Peggy and I acquired our first home, our next order of business was acquiring a dog. It just seemed a natural order of priorities. However, after eleven years of marriage, children, and dogs, I thought it would be nice to diversify. So, on our twelfth wedding anniversary, I presented Peggy with a six-month-old coatimundi.

I don't know how many readers have ever seen a coatimundi, but Amigo looked like a cross between a teddy bear, a raccoon, and an anteater. Despite his ungainly long nose, which he used as a lever and crowbar when he wanted to get into something, to me he always seemed to possess an innate quality of beauty—a quality not always apparent to strangers and certainly not apparent to Peggy on this occasion.

Unfortunately, because I had to travel clear across Detroit to pick Amigo up, I arrived at our anniversary party almost two hours late and after all the guests had arrived.

A coatimundi, even as young as six months, is not an easy thing to conceal and is impossible to gift wrap. When I walked from the foyer into the living room and confronted the stares of my family and friends, I could think of nothing more appropriate to say to my awaiting wife than, "Honey . . . this is for you."

After recovering from the initial shock, Peggy burst out in sobs. At first I couldn't imagine that my being two hours late had affected her so. I have since come to acknowledge that perhaps a sentimental occasion, such as a wedding anniversary, might better be celebrated by a gift of a less animate nature.

Before long, it became routine for Peggy and Amigo to meet me when I arrived home from work. Amigo had a voracious appetite, and in addition to the dog food and fruit that comprised his regular diet, he delighted in searching through the lawn for the little tidbits of insects or plants that his palate might savor.

As soon as I would step from my car, Amigo would come bounding across the lawn, and while still several feet away, take a giant leap into my outstretched arms. After one or two times, it became painfully obvious that his greeting was not entirely unselfish. Being an inveterate cigar smoker, I always carried several cigars in by breast pocket. Because it took both of my hands to hold on to him, I was never able to prevent the probing attack of his long snout and the subsequent loss of two or three cigars.

Changing the cigars to an inside pocket worked only temporarily. His keen sense of smell made his nose a homing device with which he could locate tobacco no matter where it was secreted.

Amigo's penchant for climbing drapes and chewing tobacco were just two of his dubious qualities that tested Peggy's limits of tolerance.

Perhaps because of his age, Amigo had seemingly boundless energy. This, plus his affinity for fun and games, eventually forced me to agree to confine Amigo while Peggy and I slept. He had brought that decision upon himself by tactlessly choosing that hour of the night when we had just fallen asleep to start playing leapfrog across our bed.

As if that was not enough, more than once Peggy was awakened from a deep sleep by the sensation that some foreign object was hovering just over her head. Sure enough, her eyes would focus in on the dark outline of Amigo hanging upside down from the bedpost with his long nose just inches from her face, watching her sleep.

Nighttime confinement was an amicable alternative to some of Peggy's other suggestions.

The first two or three attempts to keep Amigo confined failed to produce an escape-proof enclosure. My final product was almost a masterpiece of engineering. It was a cage about three feet in height, length, and depth. Because of its size, it was necessary to keep it in the basement. In anticipation of his wily deftness for getting in and out of impossible places, I secured the door with a heavy padlock. Since the cage weighed about seventy-five pounds, there appeared no reason to construct a bottom for it, as I knew he couldn't dig through the concrete floor.

But there was a reason, and it arrived in the form of my monthly shipment of Maduro Palma cigars from

Florida. On this particularly hot and humid June evening, I placed the new shipment of cigars inside my handsome walnut humidor, locked Amigo in his cage in the basement, and retired for the night.

Early the next morning, I was jolted awake by the unrestrained screams of my wife. I ran toward the family room expecting to see some unspeakable horror. Perhaps horror lies in the eyes of the beholder, for all I saw was darling little Amigo sitting up in one corner of our good couch, staring innocently up at us.

A closer inspection found his fingers and mouth stuffed with the shredded remains of one hundred Maduro Palma cigars. From one end of the room to the other, our prized sculptured orange carpet bore the remains of the rest of the cigars. Not only the carpeting, but the walls and drapes were liberally soiled with soggy, chewed tobacco. To make matters worse, the abundance of tobacco was more than poor Amigo's system could tolerate, and the carpeting and sofa bore more than just tobacco remains.

Apparently, with the proper motivation, Amigo's powerful nose had sufficient strength to lift his cage off the floor and permit his escape. Freed of our restraint, he went directly to the family room and to my cigar humidor.

Like any normal man, I cannot remain indifferent to a woman's tears. With great reluctance, I agreed that maybe Amigo would be happier in a home where there would be fewer temptations. That afternoon, I telephoned a want ad into the local newspaper. "Adorable pet coatimundi for sell or trade." After all, Peggy didn't say how I should get rid of him.

If I had had twenty coatimundis, I still would not have been able to meet the demand. If I was surprised by the number of callers, I was amazed at the variety of animals I was offered in exchange. I had no idea so many exotic pets existed outside the Detroit zoo.

My attachment for Amigo extended far beyond any monetary value, so my main concern was to find a new owner with a nature sympathetic to his peculiar behavior.

My final choice appeared to provide me the best of both worlds. Not only did the woman know all about the raising of coatimundis, but one of her rare exotic cats was pregnant, and our agreement gave me my choice of the litter. What a deal!

The litter finally arrived in late fall.

For some reason, I had neglected to tell Peggy about the terms of the deal, so I was once again bringing home an unexpected pet to an unsuspecting wife. It was a particularly cold and windy day when I arrived with a wicker basket holding a tiny bundle of striped fur. I tried to shield the basket with my coat and hold the storm door with one foot while I pushed open the front door. I was counting on at least getting into the foyer before being discovered by Peggy or the children. Unfortunately, as the door finally swung open, I could see Peggy coming to greet me.

"What's in the basket?" she asked in a suspicious tone.

"Nothing special," I answered, a bit sheepishly.

"There's got to be something in it," she said with conviction.

I set the basket on the tile floor and attempted to put my arms around her and give her a greeting kiss. Her lips avoided mine and she tilted her head to one side, her eyes glued to the wicker basket.

"What's in the basket?" she demanded more firmly.

"Well." I paused, trying to think of some way to phrase an explanation. "I brought you something."

She had stopped smiling and was standing there just staring at the motionless basket.

"It's really something special." I emphasized the word special.

Still, she didn't move, remaining in my embrace with her head tilted down toward the basket. Finally, she pushed herself out of my arms and clutched her hands tightly together. I recalled a similar reaction the first time she saw Amigo.

"It's a kitten," I explained reassuringly, hoping to head off any violent reaction. "I knew you'd like it the moment I saw it." This was stretching the truth more than a little. Peggy was not at all inclined toward cats. In fact, on a number of occasions she actually expressed a natural antipathy toward felines. The attitude had been fostered during her childhood in Finland, where

6

her mother insisted that cats were bad luck. The mere sight of a cat prompted her family and friends to make a motion of spitting, which was thought to ward off bad luck.

She moved toward the basket and knelt, watching for some kind of movement. Cautiously, her fingers began peeling back the layers of towels and rags, finally revealing a tiny ball of tricolored tufts of fur. The thing was no larger than her hand and it lay there almost motionless, with only a barely perceptible stomach movement when it breathed. Its markings bore the spotted pattern most people would associate with a leopard. On the back of each ear was a white circle amidst the dark fur. There was something very obviously different about this cat.

"What kind of cat did you say this was?" Peggy asked. Her voice had mellowed and had lost its harsh, critical quality.

"It's an ocelot," I answered. "Sort of a cat that lives in South America. They're quite common as house pets there," I added, trying to reassure her.

Although the woman who had bartered him to me in exchange for Amigo had told me this, I hadn't the slightest idea if it was true or not.

"They only get to be about twenty or twenty-five pounds—just a little larger than an ordinary house cat."

Noticing that her interest was now totally absorbed in the tiny bundle of fur, I continued on with a recitation of the virtues of owning an ocelot. Some of the things had been told me by the previous owner. Most I merely made up to embellish the prospects of ownership.

At last Peggy spoke up. "When did it eat last?" She was holding the tiny kitten level with her eyes and seemed to be studying its face. "I'll bet this thing is starving to death! Kittens this small have to be fed frequently. I don't think it's even been weaned."

I shrugged my shoulders. I hadn't really considered this. Nor could I imagine how she could be so certain of impending disaster unless it was some instinct peculiar to women. However, I could only interpret her immediate concern as a favorable omen, so I agreed and suggested that we feed the cub immediately.

7

"Feed it? Feed it what?" she asked sarcastically. "Did you bring home any Esbilac or baby formula? You can't give a little thing like this a roast beef sandwich!" Having made her point, she continued on in a more sympathetic tone. "I don't think this little guy is more than five or six weeks old. He sure doesn't look good. I wonder if it's even been fed today?"

Then, she abruptly placed the tiny figure back into the basket and covered it. "Put the basket next to the kitchen register and let's get to the store before it closes."

Once we were in the car, the serious questions started. "Who?" "How much?" "When?" "How much?" "Why?" "How much?" And, in response to any of my replies, "Don't give me that. Tell the truth!"

Still, despite all the questions and doubts, I felt a strong sense of relief that her voice lacked that certain bitter quality she was capable of expressing when she was really angry. I kept my eyes riveted on the road ahead, but inwardly I was grinning like the Cheshire Cat. I was sure she was going to accept the ocelot.

After several trips around the racks of baby foods and baby supplies, our shopping basket contained an ample collection of cereals, baby and junior foods, plus a variety of baby bottles and nipples. During the early years of our marriage, shopping was frequently an exercise in controversy. Peggy would pick an item from a shelf and then I would search the shelves for a similar product with a lower price. Then she would replace my choice with her original selection and an argument would ensue. It is a marital ritual I still see practiced whenever young couples do their grocery shopping together. It only ends when the wife learns not to include the husband in her weekly shopping excursions. On this occasion, I made no effort to audit her choice of products. If she had filled the cart with imported caviar, I wouldn't have said one word. Instead, I stood to one side, searching the store with my eyes for any signs of neighbors. I could just imagine the rumors this scene could provoke. When she was satisfied that she had everything she needed, Peggy advised me that we were now going to find a store that offered a book on how to raise ocelots.

Since I had not even known such an animal existed, I seriously doubted that we were going to find the book she described, even in a pet shop.

However, I didn't want to do anything that might affect Peggy's growing interest, so I agreed to chauffeur her from one pet shop to another until she came to the same conclusion. Fortunately, her intuition withstood the trial and by the sixth or seventh pet shop, some forty miles from our home, her perseverance was rewarded. She pulled a thin, glossy jacketed booklet from a wire rack and read the title aloud. *"How to Raise Ocelots,* by Catherine Cisin. Here it is!" she exclaimed, as if she had always known for sure it existed.

On the cover was a picture of a beautiful, sleek jungle cat. Once inside the car, Peggy opened the book and began to read the text aloud. She would pause and repeat what she felt were critical passages and then would pause again as if to allow the information to sink in. By the time we arrived back home, I think she felt she had mastered the situation and knew exactly what had to be done.

Having raised three children, Peggy prepared the bottle of baby formula as she had so many times in the past, even to the testing of the temperature by forcing a few drops from the bottle onto her wrist.

Next, she picked the small bundle of fur from its nest of torn pieces of blanket and placed it on a towel in her lap. It didn't move. Although we could see a very slight movement of its stomach with each breath, it failed to open its eyes or show any other sign of activity. Peggy pried the tiny mouth open and moved the nipple back and forth, trying to get the cub to accept it. There was no response.

"It's too weak to eat," she said, slowly turning the bottle in an attempt to evoke a response. "Get me an eye dropper."

I removed our only eye dropper from an old bottle of baby medicine and rinsed it out several times in hot water. Peggy poured some formula into an open cup and, after checking the eye dropper to be sure I had cleansed it properly, filled it with formula.

She carefully tilted the cub's head backward and drop

by drop let the formula trickle into its throat. It was a slow and tedious procedure, but Peggy was convinced the animal was on the verge of death and only an ample infusion of nourishment would save it.

While our three children looked on with obvious delight, our poor mixed Labrador retriever, Plato, didn't appear to share in the spirit of the occasion. Instead, he sniffed the new arrival and then lay down in a corner of the kitchen to watch the proceedings from afar. Perhaps, by some uncanny canine sense, Plato realized that this intruder would soon take over his place as top dog in the Leeds household.

I woke up the first two or three times Peggy got up that night to feed the cub, but I finally managed to fall into a deep sleep that was interrupted only by the alarm clock. Peggy was not in bed. I walked to the kitchen and found her seated at the table, the kitten in her lap, dripping formula down its throat with the eye dropper.

The scene was the same when I returned from work that evening.

"The formula is going down much better," she said. "You can see its tongue move now." A big smile never left her face as she related the entire day's events in detail.

I now knew that despite our first misadventure, Peggy was going to accept the ocelot. Neither of us mentioned the potential difficulties of raising such an animal. When one of the children asked a question, either Peggy or I would answer with a reply that ignored the probable problems inherent in raising a wild animal in a domestic environment.

By the third day, the cat was able to nurse from a bottle, and we all shared a sense of relief and accomplishment when it took its first wobbly steps, fell over, and then got back up and tried again. I watched Peggy's face as she urged the small bundle of fur to walk to her and when it reached her at last, we all gave a cry of joy.

The cat had managed to do more than just take a few steps. He had managed to walk into our hearts, and from that moment on became another of America's millions of pampered pets.

He was now a permanent member of the Leeds household.

# THE LESSON OF
# SOCRATES

I should have suspected this euphoria would be short-lived, for once this period of crisis passed, Peggy's innate sense of pragmatism came to the fore. The animal was, after all, an unknown quantity. Order and cleanliness were obsessions with my wife. In order for the animal to stay with us, it would have to conduct itself in accordance with the rules of the mistress of the house.

In fifteen years of married life, even I hadn't been able to satisfy her criteria for neatness and order, and I argued that such demands on a creature of the jungle were much too severe. I was pleading my case to a deaf jury. I finally conceded that certain conditions were the sacred right of the homemaker. I also recognized that the provision of certain domestic luxuries, not the least of which was her weekly batch of homemade bread, could best be assured by my concession to what was really a reasonable demand. The children and I agreed that if the animal did not conform to her expectations, he would have to go.

It was this understanding that led us to name the cat Socrates. His future was dependent upon his own actions.

Over the next five years, Socrates grew from a half-pound weakling into a lovable fifty-five-pound bundle of muscular energy. His diet of baby formula soon gave way to chicken necks, supplemented with whatever fish or meat the nearby supermarket wished to dispose of at a reduced price.

There were occasions when Socrates tested Peggy's determination, such as the time he stole our Sunday dinner. The family was watching television while a four-pound chicken was defrosting on the kitchen table. Since Socrates barely tipped the scales at one pound and logically should not have been able to gain access to the tabletop, we had no premonition of what was about to happen.

Hearing a loud thump coming from the direction of the kitchen, Peggy and I ran to investigate the noise. There, moving slowly across the kitchen floor, was our next day's dinner. Only partially visible from behind the chicken were two upright furry ears. Socrates had his teeth embedded in the partially defrosted chicken and, with all the strength he could muster, was dragging the chicken backward toward the deserted hallway.

Yet of all the foods we ever gave him, his favorite was an ordinary banana. His addiction to bananas even exceeded Amigo's fondness for tobacco. Knowing this, we soon learned always to place bananas on top of the refrigerator, where they were well beyond his reach.

With the passage of time and the subsequent disappearance of a bunch of bananas, we learned that Socrates was now able to reach the top of the refrigerator with a single leap. Upon this discovery he was endowed with the nickname Super Cat.

As he matured, he developed a different pattern of behavior with each member of the family. Never during his stay with us was he confined in a cage. We even replaced a basement pane of glass with a rubber flap that led to an outdoor fenced enclosure. Being a nocturnal animal, he appreciated the ability to get up during the night and go outside to romp.

If he was ill or otherwise not feeling well, such as the time we had him declawed and neutered, he insisted on staying in our youngest daughter's bed. Being only six years old, Gail delighted in treating Socrates like a doll and would sit for hours petting him as another child might play with a toy.

Marc, who was eight years old, was Socrates' access to the outside world. As soon as Marc arrived home from school, Socrates would begin hounding him until

Marc attached the ocelot's harness and leash and led him out into the woods, where he could climb among the trees and stalk his imaginary prey.

The process was somewhat different when winter came and the ground lay buried in snow. Then it was a veritable ordeal to get Socrates to go outside. Marc would have to catch him and carry him out to a nearby tree, then struggle to free Socrates' legs from around his own neck so he could set the cat down in the snow. Socrates would relieve himself almost as soon as he hit the ground and in one leap be back in Marc's arms.

Our oldest daughter, Leslie, was a teenager, and Socrates soon learned that his pleasures with her depended upon her changing moods. Usually he was content just to lie in her lap awaiting the arrival of the master of the house.

In addition to being a source of love and affection, Peggy seemed to represent for Socrates a pantry door. From her came all the vital requisites necessary to sustain life. At a certain time every day, Socrates would find his way to the kitchen and check his feeding dish. If Peggy was preoccupied with some other task and had forgotten to fill his bowl, or if he felt hungry even though it wasn't time for his meal, Socrates would walk behind her, gently nipping at the backs of her ankles. Never would he bite down hard enough to damage the skin, but always firmly enough to let her know that he expected food.

There finally came a time when Socrates' request for food was inopportune for Peggy, so she shooed him away by waving her hands at him and ordering him to go away. Socrates stood a few feet from her and studied her face. Then, he came back and, as before, began nibbling on the backs of her ankles. This time Peggy yelled at the cat and sent him sprawling across the floor with a sweeping motion of one foot. Again the cat paused and studied Peggy's face. Socrates then turned around, raised his tail up straight, and shot a stream of urine with unerring accuracy onto the foot that had just swiped him.

The first time this happened, we treated it as a fluke. When it happened a second time, it was Peggy's behavior that changed. From that time forward, when

Socrates nibbled at her ankle, her immediate response was to give him his food.

For me he reserved the dubious honor of sparring partner. Barely had I entered the house than he would begin his game of stalking me. He loved to sit on his haunches and provoke me by striking out with one of his forelegs until I would accept the challenge and wrestle with him. After acquiring a number of painful scratches, I finally invested in a pair of heavy leather welder's gloves into which he could sink his teeth without injuring my hands.

He would wrap his four legs around my arm and hang upside down, snarling and chewing on the rough leather. From time to time, I would forget to put the gloves away, and the next morning little more than an odd finger would remain. One of his greatest delights was to wait until I had relaxed in my favorite armchair with my newspaper. He would slink unnoticed into a position at my feet and then suddenly spring up right through the paper. After a few traumatic experiences, I learned to sense his approach and to prepare for his sudden intrusion. But, try as I might, even though I anticipated his leap, when he came through the paper it was always a bit of a surprise.

Except for close friends, most of our neighbors were totally unaware of Socrates' existence. Although we were not deliberately secretive, we did not parade him around or seek attention. However, after a while his residency became so matter of fact that we hardly considered him in our daily routine, and this led to some amusing situations.

One of these occurred when we subscribed to a water-softener service. The first few weeks the service man came to change the tank, Peggy made sure the cat was locked in a bedroom. However, on one occasion she made the mistake of asking Leslie to watch Socrates while the serviceman was in the basement. Suddenly, aware that he had been in the basement an unusually long time, Peggy went to check. She found the man standing like a statue with Socrates perched astride two water pipes directly over his head. The cat was leaning down between the pipes, licking the man's bald head.

"Your little girl asked me if I was afraid of cats and

14

I said no. I didn't know you had a leopard," the poor man explained.

Peggy apologized and explained about Socrates, stressing his docile disposition. Instead of being frightened away, the man spent a portion of each subsequent call visiting with Socrates. When he was transferred to another route, he managed to trade one of his regular customers in exchange for us and continued to service our unit until we moved to another city.

Our move to Birmingham, Michigan, meant a change of schools for each of the children. Gail could think of no better way of making new friends than to take Socrates to school for "Show and Tell."

I will never understand what led Peggy to capitulate, but one sunny morning she, Gail, and Socrates took off for the local grade school. The event was spectacular. Socrates appeared to enjoy each moment as all the children lined up and marched past the table where he sat. Unfortunately, the spectacular event turned into more of a spectacle than Peggy had bargained for when the school's nurse moved in for a closer examination. Socrates had just recovered from having his claws surgically removed, and apparently the white gown of the nurse reminded him of the veterinarian who had given him considerable pain. With one loud shriek, Socrates leaped from the table while spraying everything behind him with a diarrhetic discharge. While the children clamored for more, "Show and Tell" was brought to an abrupt halt, and Peggy and Socrates were politely urged to use the nearest exit to return home.

In July 1965, the family decided to take a vacation out West and the dilemma of finding a temporary home for Socrates arose. The local kennels were willing to board our dog, but Socrates was something else. Even the veterinarian who serviced our regular needs declined to have him as a regular guest.

I called several kennels before I found one that said their facilities were adequate to hold an ocelot. The owner not only had an attractive ad in the Yellow Pages, but also claimed to be experienced in caring for all types of exotic pets. The price was steep, but since he was the only one I could find who had experience

15

with exotics (and since no one else was willing to board Socrates at any price), I confirmed the arrangement.

Our plans called for us to leave directly after work on Saturday, so to save time we arranged to take Socrates to the kennel on Friday evening. When we arrived, a sense of foreboding came over me. The facilities were far different from the impressive structure portrayed in the ad.

The kennels were composed of several old wooden structures that had been partitioned off into pens on the inside. There was no evidence of air conditioning, but the windows were open to permit the occasional breeze to pass through. Several young children were running around yelling to the dogs to be quiet, but except for the man who met us, no other attendants were to be found.

This was the first time I realized how important it was to visit a boarding facility before leaving a pet there. Not even guessing the worst, like most pet owners I figured I had no alternative but to go ahead with the arrangement.

The kennel operator apparently sensed my disappointment and hastily sought to assure me that he had special areas within his house for special guests like Socrates.

As he had promised, the inside of the house did contain several enclosures adequate to contain Socrates with a degree of safety. There was a perceptible odor of urine emanating from the wooden partitions and floors, but except for a hot water tank and some water lines in these areas, there was ample room for Socrates to sleep and play. My apprehensions were lessened when the operator inquired about Socrates' diet requirements, and I was further relieved when I saw how the man handled and played with the cat.

While I still harbored some latent fears, since we were due to leave the following day, I convinced myself that there was no apparent alternative. With more hope than conviction, I reassured Peggy and the children that everything would be all right until we returned.

The following morning, I arrived at work to find a telephone message asking me to call the kennel immediately.

I placed the call and recognized the owner's voice when he answered the phone.

"Mr. Leeds, I'm afraid I've got some bad news."

"How bad?" I asked, aware of the multitude of things Socrates might have done.

"I'm afraid your cat is dead."

Neither of us spoke. While I could anticipate some problem, I was totally unprepared for this. I felt a large lump forming in my throat as I struggled to hold back the tears.

Finally, the man from the kennel broke the silence. "He must have climbed up on the water heater during the night and weaved in and out between the pipes. Apparently, he jumped off and the leash snagged on the pipes. We found him in the morning, hanging."

When I was able to gain a measure of composure, I asked the man how he could even think of boarding a cat with its collar and leash on. It was a stupid thing to do.

Suddenly I realized how stupid it all was. You don't have hot water tanks or any other obstruction inside an animal's enclosure. You don't board your pet in a makeshift facility that appears to be falling apart and that reeks of urine and feces. You don't board a pet you love in a kennel that compromises its care by using immature children in place of qualified attendants.

Certainly the kennel was guilty of gross neglect. But inside I knew that I was equally guilty for having boarded Socrates without first checking out the facility.

Only a person who has lost a pet can understand the depth of grief. For all of us, the loss was tragic and profound. But it would also affect our lives in a way never dreamed of at the time. Whether preordained or not, it was Socrates' needless death that caused me eventually to resign my position with General Motors and catapulted me into a venture that promised to revolutionize the entire pet-care industry.

# PET BOARDING
# IN AMERICA

One of the first questions I asked myself after Socrates' death was why there wasn't a single modern kennel in the entire Detroit area—a kennel designed and built to provide some measure of the security and comfort that a household pet enjoyed at home. Was it because there were not enough animals boarded to warrant the investment in modern, efficient facilities? Maybe the employment of children or other family members was the only way a kennel could survive in the absence of a genuine market. I doubted this was true. I couldn't believe there weren't thousands of pet owners like myself who would gladly pay a little more for the satisfaction of knowing our pets were well taken care of.

With the memory of Socrates fresh in my mind, I decided to take a look at the pet-boarding business.

For the past several years, a part of my responsibilities with GM had been the preparation of feasibility studies for new plants and products. I was well schooled to conduct an analysis of the pet-boarding industry.

My first task was to determine whether or not there was such a thing as a pet-boarding industry. To garner the necessary data, I designed and mailed out an innocuous four-page questionnaire to the eighty-one dog kennels serving the Detroit area. An analysis of the results would provide me with much of the information I required.

My market studies showed there was certainly a demand for boarding facilities. In 1965, Detroiters spent $1.67 million in boarding kennels. I was more impressed when I realized that close to that amount was also spent with veterinarians who were boarding dogs and cats in their hospital cages. This latter market was one I had entirely overlooked while doing my initial research. The results of the survey more than vindicated my impression that boarding animals was an industry. There were no more doubts in my mind. It was an industry that begged to be developed in a positive way.

Visiting kennels became a preoccupation during my free time. These personal visits did even more to firm my resolve to transform the industry than the unfortunate death of my own pet, which had spawned this obsession.

My visits revealed an industry almost totally lacking in pride or cohesiveness. Except for a handful of dedicated kennel operators, the majority were totally indifferent to the problems of the business. They were unprofessional and unscrupulous. Nonetheless, perhaps because there were too few alternatives, pet owners patronized these businesses and by so doing, encouraged their undeserved success.

Not a single kennel I visited was willing to accept any liability for the pets they boarded. On the contrary, if any kind of written boarding agreement was offered to the pet owner, it always contained the specific clause, "If your pet runs away, disappears, becomes ill, is injured or dies while boarding, we are not responsible." It seemed to me that this was a hell of a way to run a business.

The conditions I found inside those kennels that permitted me access supported the logic of a boarding agreement that denied liability for anything and everything. The exterior appearance of the kennel often was indicative of what you might expect to find on the inside, though this was not always the case. In one very nice-appearing facility, which displayed a huge sign advertising heated and air-conditioned kennels, I found the bowls of water frozen and the temperature hovering below the freezing point.

There was a space heater in the kennel, but it was not operating and did not appear adequate to cope with any degree of cold, let alone sub-zero temperatures. The conversion of garages, barns, and other outbuildings into kennels frequently resulted in the use of portable kerosene heaters that presented more of a health threat than they did a solution to the cold. The regular news reports that some kennel had burned to the ground with tragic loss of animal life was confirmation enough.

One of the largest and most successful kennels was located on a main highway in northwest Detroit. The owner never flinched when she told me that every month one or two dogs managed to escape and run out onto the highway and get killed. Apparently, the slight additional investment in a chain link security fence around the kennel was not even a consideration, despite the continuing loss of people's pets.

My fourteen-year-old son, Marc, worked for this woman during one summer vacation. The woman's two young children were the only other employees. Each day, Marc would return home and relate pathetic stories of what transpired in this "outstanding" kennel.

Like most of the kennels I investigated, this one advertised heated and air-conditioned facilities. But, as so often was the case, the equipment was seldom used because of the expense involved.

On one particular day, Marc returned home visibly upset. That morning, one of the owner's children had forgotten to open the windows in the garage, which was filled with cages of dogs, stacked one on top of the other, from the floor to the ceiling. The outside temperature hit the nineties, but inside the garage, the body heat from all those dogs raised the temperature to over one hundred degrees. By the time this was discovered, several dogs had already died, and a number of others were suffering from heat exhaustion and were near death. Marc was able to see bodies on the floor before he was chased out by the owner. It was typical of the problems that arise when immature children, instead of competent adults, are used to care for boarded animals.

As happens all too often in such cases, the kennel

owner got her own veterinarian to address a note to each pet owner stating that the cause of death was due to heart failure.

On Long Island, New York, a personable young lady who operated a grooming parlor advertised that she would board dogs in a family environment in her home. Instead of taking the dogs home, however, she had her fourteen-year-old, mentally retarded son take the dogs to the basement of her grooming parlor where they were placed in cages.

While her grooming parlor was bright and attractive, the portion of the basement in which she kept over one hundred dogs lacked even the least amenity. She was aware that her son never fed or checked the animals on weekends or holidays, but she gave no consideration to the condition of the animals unless one or more died or the stench became so bad that she had to force her son to clean the cages. On one occasion, when the odor became unbearable, she went down into the basement and found one corner of the basement filled to the ceiling with dog feces and urine-soaked newspapers.

One of her employees related the story only after he quit because he was ordered to bathe and brush out a dog that had been dead for several days so it could be given to the owner. Owners of deceased pets were always told that their dog had "keeled over from a heart attack" while being played with in her home. Pets were not even given their special medications or diets, although these were provided by the owners.

Such reports helped shape my own future employment criteria. For one thing, I resolved never to employ young, irresponsible children as animal attendants. The other resolution was that, although I would employ the services of veterinarians, any relationship would be maintained at arm's length. I would never ask a veterinarian to lie for me, and I would never work with one who was willing to do so.

The conditions and problems I discovered were not entirely unknown to the pet-owning public. Still, for some reason, few good people seemed inclined to enter the pet-boarding business with the intention of conducting it on a professional level. Even to this day, despite the tremendous growth in pet ownership, the

21

industry has remained static, with as many kennels going out of business each year as there are new kennels being built. The result is that during the summers and holidays, pet owners are forced to accept undesirable accommodations for their pets because nothing better is available. It remains the ideal trade for the unscrupulous entrepreneur.

Abuses were not only rampant among breeders and unskilled kennel operators, but, surprisingly, were common almost to the same degree among veterinarians who sought extra income by providing boarding services in addition to their medical practice. It was particularly disturbing to find educated and trained professionals guilty of all the bad practices existing in the boarding industry.

One lady who boarded her pet with her veterinarian received the dog back with one of its eyes gouged out and with over sixty stitches in its body. Apparently, the dog had been put into a cage with several other dogs, a practice called "double dipping." When the owner picked up her dog, the veterinarian advised her that he would not be responsible for the cost of any further treatment should any problems arise from these injuries. If he had to absorb the cost himself, he explained, he would be too tempted to use the cheapest drugs and treatment—and that would be against his ethics!

I have heard of numerous cases where veterinary hospitals have boarded perfectly healthy cats in cages next to cats with feline leukemia, a contagious form of cancer spread by a virus. Since the symptoms may take several years to appear, it is highly unlikely that a cat owner would ever trace the source of this killer back to the time the cat was boarded at the veterinarian's.

Numerous other diseases and ectoparasitic conditions, such as hemobartonella, coccidiosis, infectious peritonitis, conjunctivitis, toxoplasmosis, sarcoptic mange, parvovirus, and coronavirus, can be spread to a healthy animal when it is boarded in the proximity of animals carrying these disorders. The staff of every veterinary hospital is well aware of this.

When you stop and analyze the problem, it seems almost inconceivable that any pet owner would choose to board a loved pet where there are sick animals. Perhaps because the veterinarian is cloaked in the mantle of professionalism by virtue of a diploma and a white gown, many pet owners never question the wisdom of this option.

In the past, almost every veterinary association was on record opposing the boarding of healthy animals in veterinary clinics and hospitals. Still, it was done regardless of the resulting hazards to the animals' health, and today, due to the increase in the number of veterinarians and an increasing emphasis on profitability, many associations have been pressured by their members to rescind this restriction from their bylaws.

Two of the most reprehensible practices common in the pet boarding business are "double dipping" and "splitting runs."

Double dipping, also referred to as "community boarding," as already mentioned, involves placing several unrelated dogs or cats in the same pen or cage due to the lack of enough facilities. This practice necessarily leads to occasional fights and subsequent injury or even death to one or more animals.

An equally abhorrent practice is the splitting of runs, a deception common in kennels that advertise "indoor-outdoor" runs. Perhaps because they have already experienced the problems of "community boarding," these kennel owners simply lock the door between the inside run and the outside run and place one animal on each side.

The problem arises when the temperature goes into the hundreds or drops below freezing. During the worst blizzard in Chicago's history, the wind-chill factor dropped to eighty-one degrees below zero and many dogs locked outside at one of Chicago's largest kennels were found frozen to death on Christmas morning.

In Texas and other southern states, there is the opposite problem during periods of oppressively hot temperatures. The dogs locked in the outside areas and those locked in the inside of un-air-conditioned kennels are subject to strokes and death from heat prostration. The profitability of these practices, for those who do not accept liability for the pets, make them very common. A kennel with only twenty or thirty runs can board five or six times that number of animals.

At a national convention of the American Boarding Kennels Association, I was discussing the ethics of the pet-boarding industry with a kennel owner from Ohio in an attempt to define ethical behavior.

I told him about the experience a friend of mine had when he boarded his twelve-pound Yorkshire terrier. He had driven many miles to a very nice-looking rural kennel, where he was assured his dog would have its own private indoor-outdoor run.

He arrived back from his vacation two days early, and like pet owners everywhere, he headed straight for the kennel to get his dog. The lobby was jammed with people bringing their pets in for the upcoming weekend.

When he asked for his dog, he could see the color drain out of the owners' faces. My friend followed one of them to an adjoining office where the man began looking among a dozen small cat-carrying cases until he found the one he was looking for.

He opened the front panel and the dog's head poked cautiously out. Suddenly, he bolted past them and ran to the lobby exit door where, literally screaming, he tried to claw his way out of the building.

Apparently, the dog had spent the better part of two weeks cramped into a cat-carrying case that was so small he could barely stand up in it. There is no way to be certain, but it is likely the dog had been forced to eat, sleep, and eliminate, all in that tiny container.

The operators of this "nice-looking" kennel were just like many other kennel operators. They tell the pet owner his dog will have a spacious indoor-outdoor run, but as soon as the owner is out of sight, the dog is put into another run in which several dogs are already being kept, or it is shoved into some kind of container. The "spacious indoor-outdoor" run is then rented to the next unsuspecting pet owner.

The kennel operator I was telling the story to was shaking his head from side to side.

"That was unethical," he said. "They should have at least built a wall so people couldn't see into their office."

The prevailing joke in the pet-boarding business is that "animals never tell."

I continued my research into every aspect of pet boarding for four years after the death of Socrates. The investigations and studies were organized and completed with the same thoroughness I would have used had I been studying the merits of a major project for General Motors.

I used every available free moment to visit kennels and animal research facilities throughout the country. Ralston Purina, Quaker Oats, Carlson Research Institute at the University of Chicago, and dozens of other institutions were all kind enough to permit me to inspect their facilities and to discuss the problems of pet boarding.

I initiated acquaintanceships with as many veterinarians and kennel operators as I could, soliciting information. More often than not, I detected a slight tinge of resentment if I revealed my intentions to these people. Over and over again, I was assured that the investment of substantial monies in a pet-boarding facility was folly. "The mass boarding of all types of animals is impossible." "Too many viruses." "Too many bacterial infections." "Too many unsolvable problems." "It has been tried before and always failed." My dream was already someone else's nightmare.

I was thoroughly tutored in the industry's faults, and despite assurances that nothing could be done about them, I was still convinced that remedies were available. Good pet care *was* possible, and I was going to prove it was economically feasible.

# THE PERFECT
# PET CARE FACILITY

There were no school courses or textbooks available on how to build or operate a kennel. Even the state's Department of Agriculture, which had jurisdiction over pet-boarding facilities, could not offer a single printed document to guide a newcomer to the industry. There was no trade association, nor were there any trade magazines from which a person might learn. It was no wonder problems were common and had persisted over the years.

The Director of the Carlson Research Institute did offer me a government pamphlet that included the recommendations of the Committee on the Guide for Laboratory Animal Facilities and Care of the Institute of Laboratory Animal Resources, National Academy of Sciences–National Research Council. In addition, I contacted the Government Printing Office and obtained copies of all congressional acts that pertained to animal welfare.

Although this information related to animal research facilities and to the interstate transportation of animals, it at least offered data on ventilation and sanitation that weren't available elsewhere. While some of these requirements might be thought of as being too severe for a commercial facility, I felt their incorporation would only add to the safety and welfare of my guests. The recommendations of the National Academy of Sciences became a part of our specifications.

After interviewing several architects, I made my selection and contracted for the development of a formal set of plans and specifications for a four-hundred-room pet motel that would serve as a model to anyone in the business, as well as to anyone wanting to enter the profession.

To start with, I concentrated on dealing with the problem of stress. From all of the information I garnered, there was one common area of agreement. Stress was responsible for more illnesses and deaths among boarded pets than any other single factor. With young animals, it led to enteritis and dehydration. With older animals, it contributed to kidney failure.

To remedy this problem, a separate area was designed for each type of pet. Only dogs were to be kept in the kennels. Cats were to be housed in four-foot-high "apartments," in two separate catteries. Not only couldn't they see the dogs, but they wouldn't even be able to hear them. There are many homes where a dog and cat live together in complete harmony, but this is a learned condition and not natural. As a rule, when a dog comes into the proximity of a strange cat, the natural tendency is for the two animals to display a strong animosity toward each other. The result is an abnormal degree of stress in both animals.

I have been in many kennels and veterinary hospitals where the cats are enclosed in portable cages and stacked on top of the dog runs in the kennels. The dogs bark continuously at the cats, and the cats scream back their own peculiar whine of defiance. When the pet owner calls for his pet, he gets back a neurotic animal that will take months to straighten out, if ever.

Since the problem of stress was a major consideration for all species, our design had to recognize that not just dogs and cats, but all animals with a natural hostility toward each other would never be boarded in the same area. Besides kennels and catteries, separate facilities would include an aquarium, aviary, serpentarium, stable, and a small-animal room, our "Bunny Club."

Each area was designed to hold a specific number of animals without overcrowding. Special ventilation systems would provide up to twenty complete fresh air changes an hour while maintaining comfortable temperatures during the most extreme weather conditions.

Published studies indicating dogs and cats relax when serenaded by soothing music (and appeared agitated when exposed to hard-rock music) prompted us to incorporate a special communications system that would carry soft music to every pet area, both inside and out. A master control in the manager's house would permit him to monitor each animal area with the push of a button.

Since dog boarding would constitute the largest portion of our business, most of the innovations were directed toward dogs.

To reduce stress further and to permit the kind of care I felt was desirable, the plans included dividing the dog facilities into five separate kennels, with no kennel containing more than fifty dog runs. The Imperial Kennel was further subdivided into three areas. A center section with four extra-large rooms measuring six feet square was called the Regency Suite and the two adjoining areas, the Imperial suites, each contained nineteen rooms.

The Imperial and Regency suites were designed to offer special provisions for those pets whose owners wanted more than conventional boarding care.

Each dog's room would be equipped with wall-to-wall Astroturf carpeting, a miniature brass bed, a foam rubber mattress, and fresh sheets each day. Because each attendant would have only a few dogs to take care of, extra time could be allocated for brushing or playing with each dog. While all the dogs would receive a treat of Milk Bones before being locked in at night, dogs in the Imperial and Regency suites would receive an extra "cookie-break" in the afternoon.

The idea of a two-tier level of care was not part of my original planning but was incorporated after a number of prospective customers convinced me that people like themselves would never board their dogs in a conventional kennel. If I had known how many people would desire and pay for this kind of care, I would have provided more Imperial and Regency suites than Deluxe suites. The additional charge of two dollars a day was no barrier, regardless of the pet owner's economic status. Love and concern for their pets were the criteria. In later years, the Imperial and Regency suites would be booked as much as a year in advance for summers and major holidays.

The demand for additional services eventually led to the installation of telephones in the Regency suites so owners could call their pets. When the pet owner telephoned the motel, his or her call could be switched to the dog's suite, where the attendant could plug in a Mickey Mouse telephone and hold the receiver to the dog's ear. Although our pets received telephone calls from all over the world, the distinction for the most expensive call has to go to a Chicago businessman who, while he was aboard a cruise ship in the Caribbean, telephoned his dog every day. Each time, he would urge the receptionist to hasten the connection to his dog's room because the call was costing him eighteen dollars and fifty cents a minute. Only a pet owner can understand these kinds of amenities. For those with doubts, let me assure you that dogs definitely recognize their owner's voice over the telephone or on a tape recording. I have seen the proof.

In almost every instance, the dog will get highly excited and begin looking around for the source of the voice. You can even note the excitement in some dogs when they see the telephone being brought into their room. They behave like a young child awaiting an expected call from a parent.

Judging by the cassette tapes we have played, I suspect most telephone conversations are filled with tender expressions of affection, although in one case I'm not sure what the owner might have told her pet to evoke the kind of response we got. After hanging up the receiver, our attendant left the room for a few minutes. When she returned, she found that the dog had chewed the telephone line into a hundred pieces. It was embarrassing to explain to our local telephone representative why we needed a new extension cord.

The establishment of different classes of boarding accommodations, with their varying charges, might seem to conflict with my original desire of offering only inexpensive boarding to the public, and when we finally opened the pet motel, it is true that the newspapers and television played up our Imperial and

Regency boarding and how much a person could spend if all the available services were ordered. Yet at the same time, people were calling us and expressing surprise that our regular boarding rates were lower than what they were paying to have their pets kept in a cage somewhere else.

A lower boarding cost was one of the virtues of the mass-boarding concept. By boarding a large number of animals, we were able to offer better care and facilities at a lower cost and still make a good profit. Besides, there was another element I wanted to build into the concept. I am firmly convinced that no job is worth anything if you don't enjoy it. I intended to have fun with mine.

When the lobby was designed, I included a mailbox for every pet's room. Pet owner's children would be invited to write to their pets, being assured that the postcards or letters would be read to them. Over the years, we have received thousands of cards and letters from all over the world, and in every case, one of our animal attendants sits down with the pet and reads the letter aloud—after allowing it to sniff the paper first. We ask that the writer sleep on the stationery before mailing it so the animal will pick up his owner's scent. In many instances, the behavior of the pet confirms that it associates the letter with its owner. It has turned out that 90 percent of the letters are from adults rather than children, but it makes no difference to us.

In some cases, the pet owners use the occasion to advise us of changes in their plans, giving pick-up dates or requesting that the animal be bathed or groomed on a different date. Some of the letters are quite serious, expressing deep affection and concern and reassuring the pet that it has not been abandoned or is not loved any less because its owner had to leave it behind. Other letters are hilarious and exhibit the unique talents of their authors.

A classic one consisted of a series of clippings glued to the paper, like a kidnapper's ransom note.

"Porkchop," the note read, "our plans have changed. Get your haircut Monday. Will spring you February 11. Be at main gate at 9 A.M. Getaway car will be in parking lot. [Signed] You know who."

In addition to giving all of us a good laugh, the note let us know the dog was going to be picked up one day later than originally scheduled and permitted us to have the dog groomed by nine o'clock.

We had our fun, too. When the owners called for their pets, the receptionist played along and said something like, "Gee. I don't know how Porkchop knew you were coming, but he has been all dressed and standing by his gate since eight o'clock." Occasions like this help justify the extra time and effort expended by both the pet owner and by us.

Of course, there have been times when a pet receives three or four scribbled letters every day of its stay from one or more children in the family, and I always wonder if the parents are as amused with the postage cost as we are with the letters' contents.

Sometimes we do certain things for our customers that we don't advertise. We would be overwhelmed if we tried to do these things for everyone. One example is the answering of letters written to a pet by a child or a pet owner who will be away for an extended period of time. Either Marc or I will sit down and draft a letter, written as if the pet itself was writing. Rover might complain about the monotony of the food and a neighbor who snored, but will always assure the owner that he is enjoying his vacation at the pet motel. Of course, the letter will always close with an expression of how much Rover misses his owners and will urge them to take good care of themselves so they can see each other soon. These letters often include a Polaroid picture of the pet.

From the beginning, these were the kind of amenities that distinguished our pet motel from a typical kennel.

To reduce stress further, each dog's room had an attached private outdoor patio. In the morning, a sliding guillotine door could be raised and the dog, passing through a hanging flexible rubber flap, could go in and out by itself. At night, or during periods of extreme temperatures, the dog could be locked inside when the sliding door was lowered. We considered this ability to go inside or outside at its own volition one of the most important considerations to a dog's health. With few exceptions, every dog is a clean animal and is "housebroken" by its own natural instinct.

Many kennels and veterinarians who keep dogs in cages or inside pens will tell you that the dogs are taken outside when they have to eliminate. Unless they board only a few dogs, or have several attendants who do nothing but constantly take the dogs outside, this is not true, nor is it possible. No kennel operator in the world knows when each animal has to eliminate. The result is that the animal restrains itself until it is ready to burst and then eliminates in its cage or pen. There are many times during the year when access to distinct toilet areas is inaccessible due to long periods of rain or snow, and it is obvious that the animals in these boarding facilities are being forced to eliminate in the same cage or pen in which they eat and sleep.

With our system of indoor-outdoor runs, we are able to board puppies, and on numerous occasions we send them home housebroken. It requires no training on our part at all. The puppies only need the ability to go outside whenever their systems require it.

The outside runs were to be covered by sturdy aluminum canopies that extended five feet past the end of the run. Aluminum has one major advantage over plastic or steel: it reflects heat. From the time these canopies were installed, we have never had a single incidence of heat prostration. Many dogs boarded in kennels that do not provide protection from the sun are not so fortunate.

Another advantage of having canopies is that the dogs can go outside even if it is raining or snowing, without getting wet. It means that the dogs stay dry and clean during their boarding, eliminating the compulsory bath imposed by many boarding facilities.

An obvious fault of many kennels is the separation of areas by only some form of wire fencing. Many times I have observed a male dog lift his leg and urinate through the wire partition, striking the dog in the next run. This is one of the reasons dogs go home from some kennels reeking of urine.

To avoid this problem and also to diminish the amount of barking, we designed our inside and outside run walls to be constructed of forty-two-inch-high concrete block, with chain link fencing going up another three feet. This design offered each dog the security he needed while still permitting good ventilation.

Drawing on the material gathered during my four years of research, many types of industries were called upon to contribute their expertise for the problems we knew existed.

One of America's leading paint manufacturers offered us a special epoxy paint for the concrete walls that would not absorb urine or succumb to acid erosion. We liked the fact that it was available in various colors but, more important, it formed an impenetrable shield over the concrete so bacteria, fleas, and larvae could not germinate in the millions of tiny crevices. Since this was a vital concern, the epoxy was included in our specifications.

A high-technology firm in California offered us some newly developed units that, when installed in incoming air ducts, would charge the particles in the air with a negative charge.

This was an interesting proposal. We were sure that our special high-pressure sterilizing system would minimize the risk of bacterial infection, but viral infections were something else. We could kill the bacteria, but viruses tend to float in the air, carried by dust or other airborne particles.

Theoretically, if we charged all the air particles with electrons, instead of floating around from animal to animal, the virus-carrying particles would be drawn to the floor by the positively charged earth, resulting in a germ-free environment. All we then had to do was to mop our floors with an effective virucide. Another benefit is that bacteria cannot survive in such a negative environment. We can leave moist foods in the animals' rooms without fear of it getting moldy or spoiling.

A further purported advantage being claimed at that time in some of the medical journals was that mental patients placed in a negatively charged environment tended to be more relaxed. If we could achieve the same results with animals, it would support our effort to reduce stress. The units were added to our plans.

More common hazards were easier for us to deal with. Every year, thousands of dogs suffer broken teeth, lacerated jaws, and even broken jaws by getting their teeth enmeshed in the chicken wire or chain link fencing most kennels use to separate one dog area from another. Chicken wire, hog wire, and most kinds of farm fencing are treacherous for commercial boarding facilities enclosures.

To prevent these types of injuries, special nine-gauge, one-and-one-half-inch mesh chain link fencing was specified for our gates. In theory, it should have worked. In practice, our canine adversaries proved it wasn't a sure thing.

Many times over the years, dogs have been able to twist, tear, and distort the chain link portions of their gates into unbelievable masses of twisted and shredded wire. The replacement of fencing became an ordinary, recurring expense. Fortunately, the two additional chain link fences that surrounded the kennels proved to be an obstacle to escape. Except in one case.

He was not the kind of dog you would expect to be the exception. A small, thirty-pound mixed terrier, this dog literally chewed through the nine-gauge steel wire to gain his freedom. When he came to the seven-foot-high perimeter fence, he dug an escape tunnel in the frozen ground and went under the lower steel bar. We saved the broken strands of steel because we doubted anyone, especially the owner, would believe a dog could perform such a feat.

Fortunately, the story had a happy ending. The dog defied capture and continued to elude us by hiding in the fields surrounding the motel. During this time, the temperature dropped below freezing, but he refused to allow anyone to come near him, nor would he come into our fenced area for food or shelter. Four days later, the dog was found sitting on the front steps of his house some six miles from the pet motel. He was surely an exceptional dog.

The constant availability of water is another important consideration for most animals, and it can be a matter of life or death for older dogs whose kidneys are beginning to deteriorate. Our solution to this concern was a special watering device manufactured by a company on the East Coast, a water bowl that was connected to a separate water system. As a dog drank from its bowl, the water would be continually replenished.

Every dog would always have as much fresh water available as it desired.

Because most dog owners object to having their dogs sleep on concrete, I decided to place a special perforated, pure vinyl matting in every dog's room. The matting we selected had risers molded into the lower surface to permit the circulation of air so the floor would dry rapidly. At a later date, we decided to add fiberglass resting pallets in the deluxe rooms, where brass beds and mattresses weren't available.

Recognizing that some dogs would use the carpets to satisfy their urge to chew on something, we had to be careful to select a carpet that was impervious to urine and bacteria and that was also nontoxic if swallowed. These parameters narrowed the alternatives and substantially increased the cost of the material selected.

Whether outside dog runs should be poured concrete or gravel is an age-old controversy that has been argued at length by persuasive advocates of each material. Although it is much cheaper to use gravel, we chose poured concrete slabs, as concrete can be cleaned and sanitized, eliminating the harboring of residue that can cause disease and infection.

The inside room sizes were a special concern of mine. I had always hated to see any kind of animal cooped up in a constrictive cage. To me, it always seemed the animal was being imprisoned or punished, rather than humanely housed. I insisted that every animal have plenty of space to move around in. That meant a sleeping area for dogs of from twelve to thirty-six square feet and an adjoining outdoor run of twelve or sixteen feet in length, depending on the size of the dog.

The threat of viral infections also had to be coped with. A single outbreak could jeopardize the health of every animal in the facility. For this reason, our heating and cooling systems had to take this risk into consideration.

Radiant heat offered the advantage of warm floors, but it failed to provide the necessary air movement we desired. To meet the Academy of Science's recommendations, we had to be able to provide up to twenty air changes an hour. In addition, we had to be able to switch to 100 percent fresh outside air if a viral infection broke out. Only a forced air ventilating system could meet these requirements.

As an added safety factor, separate heating and air-conditioning sources were installed for each animal area. This meant that we could maintain different temperatures and percentages of fresh air for each different species of animal.

The boarding of cats presented a unique set of challenges. Because of their susceptibility to viral infections, many kennels refuse even to board them. The problem is that cats can appear perfectly healthy but still be carrying one or more viruses in their systems. When they get into a stressful situation, such as when they are boarded, the stress causes changes in their metabolism, and the next thing you know, you have a sick cat who can spread its illness to every other cat in the area.

The seriousness of the hazard was heightened for me when I visited the Ralston Purina research facilities just outside St. Louis. There I learned that a recent viral outbreak had just ravaged their feline research colony, resulting in the deaths of several hundred cats.

It was a devastating blow to the world's largest pet food manufacturer. In developing their foods, detailed records had been kept on the type and quantity of food each cat and its succeeding generations had eaten. The continuing history of every imaginable breed had been carefully documented to reveal any relationship between various health problems and the cats' diets. Taste preferences and consumer attitudes had all been factored into these years of research to permit Purina to produce their quality products.

Now, with one single outbreak, the entire population had been decimated. Years of study and scientific observations were hopelessly interrupted. Those cats that survived the disease were no longer suitable for research, and a storm of controversy arose when it was learned that they were euthanized to make way for an entirely new population of feline subjects. The destruction of the surviving cats was a black eye Purina still wears in the opinion of some cat owners.

It was the construction of their new cattery that interested me, however, but their recent experience had led to the imposition of new rules and restrictions that totally forbade visitors from entering the new facilities.

Our guide at Ralston Purina's research facilities was Dr. James Corbin, the director. It was he who had been primarily responsible for the development of pelletized dog food and for Purina's dominance in the dog food industry.

Dr. Corbin turned out to possess the unique talent of being genuinely liked by everyone who meets him. Rarely have I met anyone in the pet industry who doesn't know Dr. Corbin, and I have yet to meet anyone who doesn't respect and admire him. As he guided my wife and me through the research facilities, it was easy to understand why people are impressed by him. At that time, I was still a novice and had a great deal to learn. Dr. Corbin, despite his heavy schedule, took the time and effort to explain every little detail he thought would contribute to our success. In addition to the tour, he ran several research films for us on nutrition, diseases, and the general care of dogs and cats. When we finally departed, we were loaded with pamphlets and research results that would help us in our future efforts.

Since Purina could never be sure whether the virus that wiped out their cattery had been carried in by a visitor or contracted by an airborne germ while the cats were in an outside run, both potential hazards were eliminated when they planned their new cattery. Their new building was totally enclosed and admittance was restricted to those employees who worked there. The employees were even required to wear white gowns, which were changed whenever they left or reentered the cattery.

A totally new population of disease-free cats was flown in from England on specially chartered aircraft. Once the cats entered the new facilities, they would live the balance of their lives within those walls. Every ounce of food and water would be measured and documented, and when their lives finally ended, an autopsy would reveal any characteristics that might indicate a deficiency or benefit attributable to their diet. Few pet owners realize the extent of time, effort, and money major pet food manufacturers expend on perfecting the nutritious diets pets require. It was our experience at Purina that convinced us to use only the best brands of pet food in our motels.

Purina's new facilities also incorporated a system of 100 percent fresh air. This meant that there was no recirculation of air at all. Regardless of the outside temperature, clean, fresh air was brought in, heated or cooled to the desired temperature, and then exhausted directly to the outside. Considering the temperature extremes of the St. Louis area, this had to be a very expensive alternative to any conventional ventilating system. Still, it was the only system that could assure that a virus would not be recirculated through the ventilating system over and over again, until every cat was infected.

The concept made such sense that we incorporated it into our own plans. We would be able to boast that ours was the only commercial cattery in the world with a negatively charged, 100 percent fresh air system, with all incoming air sterilized by ultraviolet light.

What we didn't contemplate at the time was the staggering increases in natural gas and electric rates after 1977 that would increase our utility bills to over $6,000 a month and threaten our very survival.

To make our rule of barring visitors from entering our catteries more acceptable, we placed a huge picture window in the wall so cat owners could observe their cats from the lobby. Most cat owners were content with this and with our explanation of the reason for the limited access. Others, however, only became more suspicious and more insistent on being allowed to enter the rooms.

Looking at your pet through a glass window doesn't tell you the level of odors or the room's temperature. We decided that the risk was outweighed by the cat owner's sense of security, so owners who wanted to were permitted to accompany their cats into the cattery. After what I had learned about the deceptions being practiced in the pet-boarding industry, I made it a cardinal rule that every pet owner had the right to see where his pet was going to be kept. I also made it an unbreakable policy that anyone, pet owner or visitor, could tour our facilities at any time during our normal operating hours. Few boarding facilities extend this offer even to their best clients.

Instead of using the standard eight-cubic-foot cage used for cats by most kennels and veterinarians, we elected to design our own cat apartments. They ranged in size from sixteen to thirty-two cubic feet, up to four times the space normally provided.

In addition, each cat apartment was equipped with at least one four-foot-high carpeted scratching post and two carpeted jump shelves on which to play and sleep.

To eliminate even the suspicion of cage-boarding, a policy was instituted that cages were never even to be stored near our boarding areas, except in the grooming parlor, where they were used for drying pets, or in one of the small-animal rooms, where they were appropriate for holding these smaller pets.

Although we did not anticipate boarding many birds, a different set of considerations dictated the accommodations within the aviary. The biggest consideration was a warm, draft-free environment without widely fluctuating temperatures. To cover a variety of possible contingencies, we planned only enough fresh air to keep the area smelling fresh and installed radiant electric baseboards for heat. In addition, a bank of radiant heat lamps was suspended from a track on the ceiling, permitting us to maintain different temperatures in different areas of the aviary.

This innovation proved most amenable for Charlie, a large Amazon parrot who became one of our regular boarders. Charlie suffered from arthritis, and we found that by pointing one of the heat lamps at one corner of his cage, we provided him with some relief for his pain. Charlie appeared to find this accommodation most welcome and basks in the heat regularly during his numerous visits.

Because we felt the aviary, with its many brilliantly plumed birds, would be a decorative feature, we located it right off the main lobby with a floor-to-ceiling glass wall through which visitors could observe the birds.

Two smaller rooms were planned for the boarding of small animals and reptiles. It was a mistake for me not to anticipate fully how many rabbits, ferrets, raccoons, monkeys, lizards, turtles, and other small animals are kept as household pets. During holidays and summers, these rooms would be filled to capacity.

A special area was designed for the boarding of fish and other aquatic guests. Space was provided for ten thirty-gallon glass aquarium tanks that could have their temperatures and filtration controlled either from a central source or individually.

Another feature that we wanted to include was a bathing and grooming salon. Not content just to have another damp cement area with someone's cast-off bathtub, I asked the architect to design a room that would have the same appearance as a beauty salon. This he did, with walls that sported red and gold flocked wallpaper and oval gold-framed mirrors. Outside the doorway was a rotating, lighted barber pole that displayed pictures of dancing poodles. Above the doorway, we placed the admonition, IF YOUR DOG IS UNBECOMING TO YOU, IT SHOULD BE COMING TO US in large white letters.

One small addition I insisted on was a master temperature controller on the dog's bathwater line. This request came about out of my own contempt for every home shower system I had ever owned. It seemed that whenever I got into a shower, someone, somewhere, would start running water, resulting in my shower water temperature alternating between scalding and freezing.

I could at least yell out at someone, but the poor dogs and cats would be at the mercy of the groomer, who might or might not take the time to adjust the faucets. With the automatic temperature modulating valve, the temperature of the shower water would never vary by more than one or two degrees from a very comfortable one hundred degrees.

After seeing the system in operation, I vowed that if I ever became wealthy, I would have a similar convenience installed in my own home.

Since the process of grooming dogs holds a certain fascination for pet owners, I asked that the grooming salon, with wall-to-wall glass partitions, be located off the main lobby. This was not only for the sake of appearance, but would serve as an additional assurance to pet owners, as dog grooming is another business whose reputation has suffered from bad practices, both real and imagined.

I decided that one way to eliminate totally the chance of a groomer abusing an uncooperative dog was to expose the process to the public. This is a good idea in theory, but on more than one occasion our image has been tarnished by the unanticipated outbursts of frustrated groomers while a lobby full of people was looking on in consternation.

A spacious three-stall horse stable and a large storage building completed the design.

When we had finished our final building plans, I was satisfied that they offered the finest option in pet boarding in America, and perhaps in the world. The buildings would not only be attractive and functional, but they would include the systems necessary to meet or exceed the recommendations set forth by the American Academy of Sciences for an animal research facility.

It was an impressive dream, but its price would be even more impressive.

# 5

# THE QUEST FOR
# FINANCING

"A quarter of a million dollars?" I gasped.

"If you compromise some of the design and don't start adding or making changes."

"My God," I intoned irreverently. "A hundred thousand. Even a hundred and fifty thousand. But two hundred and fifty thousand dollars?"

My enthusiasm was suddenly dampened by the cold realism of financial inevitability. Figuring in another $50,000 for land and site work, and we were talking $300,000. A third of a million dollars for a fancy dog kennel. In 1969, this was a lot of money, and even my best friends cautioned it was a ridiculous prospect.

I went back to my financial projections. The price tag of $300,000 appeared staggering, but when the bottom line was in place, the concept still showed I could earn a return of over 30 percent on my investment. As an engineer, I had confidence in the empirical data I had collected during my years of research. I refused to be swayed by the logic of those less familiar or by the prejudice of those more experienced.

Despite the fact that there were eighty-one boarding kennels serving the Detroit area, grossing $1.6 million dollars each year, 95 percent of these kennels had to turn away business during the holiday periods and summers. Many of these kennels required reservations weeks in advance. The demand for kennel space was there.

The facts seemed so clear, all I had to do was lay them before my friendly neighborhood banker and walk off with the needed funds.

With a briefcase full of statistics, I began making the rounds of Detroit's major banks. I went to the one that had large billboards all over the city proclaiming, "Come to us for your next million." Either it was because I didn't have my first million or possibly because they didn't have a pet motel in mind when they thought up that slogan, but in any event I came away emptyhanded.

After the first few refusals, I felt a little sorry for the bankers. After all, they were going to miss out on the opportunity of a lifetime. Then, when I ran out of banks, my sympathies lay a little more with me than with them. I began to wonder what it took to get a bank loan. Obviously, something more than a pet motel.

There were three formidable obstacles that I couldn't overcome. First, the idea of a pet motel was new. No one had ever attempted to build one, let alone succeeded at it. Second, if the business failed, the banks felt they would have trouble finding a buyer for the unusually shaped buildings (unless the buyer had friends who liked to bowl.)

The last obstacle was my lack of collateral. I was still employed with General Motors, but most of my wages and savings had been eaten up by research and architects' fees. The only property I owned was our house in Bingham Farms and that already had a sizeable mortgage. Obviously, a bank wasn't going to be the solution to the problem.

Mortgage companies were no more perceptive than banks, and after canvassing them in vain, I began the long and exhaustive march to the venture capitalists. For two years I walked from office to office, extolling the financial and humanitarian virtues of a new concept in pet boarding.

Almost without exception, the response was the same. They were impressed with the amount of detailed research and the quality of the presentation. They called their associates in to see my unique idea—an idea so different that they didn't want to be involved in the initial start-up venture. It was of little comfort that each one gave me the same assurance. "You build the first unit, and if it's as profitable as you predict, we'll loan you the money to expand."

Hell, if I had the money to build the first pet motel, I wouldn't have been there. With every rejection, my own confidence in the concept increased. The only alternative left was private financing.

Wealthy people don't have to take risks, but some do. Some do it for the prospect of exceptional monetary gain. And some do it for the excitement of creating a success out of nothing more than a bare idea. Unfortunately, the latter are few and far between.

One attribute seemed common to both types. Having already achieved financial success, they presume a divine right to amend, alter, and/or revise anything they touch. Research, market studies, and facts are set aside, and their intuition shapes the concept. Holding the purse strings conveys this right.

A perfect example were my negotiations with a group of six businessmen in Southfield, a wealthy suburb of Detroit. Two of the members were brothers who had a joint law practice. After months of reviewing documents and making compromises (mostly on my part), everyone was agreed. The contracts would be signed as soon as the two lawyers returned from a vacation in the Bahamas.

Two weeks later, I showed up for the signing only to find an almost deserted office. Only the two brothers were present. Surprise must have registered on my face, because one of the brothers immediately started explaining.

"We thought it over and since we only need three hundred thousand dollars, my brother and I are going to finance the project alone." He added that they expected to exercise 86 percent of the voting rights.

I didn't mind their taking 86 percent of the profits, but giving that much voting power to two brothers, and attorneys at that, raised certain apprehensions about my future prospects. This was especially so because these two men had been the most difficult to deal with of the original six investors.

Fortunately, or unfortunately, as the meeting wore on, it became more and more apparent that the two men had different ideas about what American Pet Motels should be.

"Look here," the older brother began. "There are some things we're just not going to do. I just got done spending two weeks in Nassau, and I met this veterinarian who made a lot of sense. There's no way we should board cats. They're just trouble. Also, it's stupid to spend money on stables and aviaries. The money is in dogs. That's what we're going to board. Dogs!"

After having spent months discussing the concept of all-pet boarding, I wasn't sure I heard him correctly. Over and over, I had stressed that if it walked, crept, crawled, slithered, swam, or flew, American Pet Motels would board it. It was the sole major distinction between a pet motel and an ordinary kennel.

The other brother picked up a thick set of prepared contracts and set them down in front of me. Then he offered me his pen.

I just sat there not believing what was happening.

"Look," the other brother said. "We've got the money. With us you'll get your pet motel. Without us you've got nothing."

In that brief moment I knew the chemistry was totally wrong. No deal at all was better than a bad compromise. Why trade a headache for an upset stomach? If they were willing to show me their muscle this early in the game, I knew what I might expect every time a tough decision had to be made.

I shook my head back and forth and began stuffing my documents back into my briefcase. Out of the corner of my eye I could see the smiles disappear from their faces. At the doorway, I turned around to see two men staring at me in seeming disbelief. One of them was still offering the pen in his outstretched hand.

"I'm sorry," I said. "It has to be a pet motel. I really haven't any interest in running a dog kennel."

The next year was spent in negotiations with the owners of one of America's largest breweries. The process might have been expedited if I could have met with them in person, but all of our correspondence had to be conducted through their attorney. They would send their questions to their attorney and he would

45

forward them to me. Then, I would send the answers to the attorney and he would forward them to his clients.

The financial Ping-Pong went on for over a year until, just when I thought everything was all set, I got the bad news. "With the stock market down so much, now wouldn't be a good time for my clients to sell any stock in order to go into this investment. However, as soon as the market comes back, my clients would be interested."

My experience in the brokerage business convinced me that there are only two kinds of people who keep all their money tied up in stock: the kind who will never sell in a declining market because they don't want to take a loss, and the kind who never sell when the market is going up because they expect more profits.

What I needed was someone who had all his money tied up in cash.

# CHICAGO, THE PROMISING LAND

By December 1970, I had exhausted my list of capital resources in Detroit without success. There were a lot of compliments on a fantastic idea and an outstanding presentation, but nobody wanted to be first.

Working six and seven days a week at General Motors didn't leave me a lot of time to devote to raising capital, and I began blaming my failure on my lack of free time. As the Christmas season approached, I came to the conclusion that I was going to have to leave General Motors. Convincing Peggy of this was not going to be that easy.

I began the softening-up process at once. Chicago suddenly became the only solution to the dilemma of raising the capital we needed. Every chance I had, I pointed out that Chicago was the best source of venture capital. She learned that it was the hub of commerce and the center of industry. It was the genesis of opportunity and the wellspring of enterprise. It was the Promised Land. I did everything except hire the elephants and a marching band to build up the necessary enthusiasm to overwhelm her ties to our present circumstances.

By the end of the year, we were both psyched into selling our dream house and striking out for Chicago, and in December 1970, I resigned from GM and we piled the last of our personal items into the car and followed the moving van out of Bingham Farms.

Only our youngest daughter, Gail, was moving with us. Leslie, our oldest daughter, was married and living in Florida, while Marc, with the support of our neighbors, prevailed upon us to let him remain with them so he could graduate from high school with all of his old friends. He neglected to mention that he and his friends planned on enlisting in the Air Force upon graduation.

Instead of purchasing a comparable home in one of Chicago's prestigious suburban communities, we decided on a small, unpretentious house in a Levitt-built subdivision, some thirty miles northwest of Chicago's loop.

Our new home was a great disappointment to Peggy. She had grown accustomed to the privacy she so much enjoyed in Bingham Farms. Even though this new house was on a cul-de-sac, with an extra large lot, it seemed as if we could reach out and touch our neighbors. The neighborhood swarmed with children who appeared at the first dawn of light and who disappeared just as mysteriously with the setting sun. They spilled over into our yard, and when they were gone, they left a trail of tricycles, toys, and clothing that sometimes remained for days before being claimed.

Instead of awakening to the sounds of birds, it was the honking of horns from neighbors' car pools. Each new day brought a parade of little cherubic figures collecting for this cause or that. With frequent regularity, neighbors who never spoke to us when we passed them on the sidewalk accosted us at our front door, urging us to sign petitions against every conceivable evil except that of distributing petitions.

We were in the real suburbs, but it was not the peaceful nature center we had enjoyed in suburban Bingham Farms, and even my constant assurance that it was only a temporary situation did little to mollify Peggy's growing disappointment.

To make matters worse, Chicago did not turn out to be the financial wellspring I had anticipated. In most instances, pleas for venture capital brought the same response I had encountered in Detroit. "You build the first pet motel and, if it's successful, we'll furnish you the capital for the second one."

During these months, I had met several people who expressed an interest in putting money into the project. But I could account for only half the monies needed. The problem was where to obtain the balance.

What happened next was one of those acts of providence.

While sitting in a friend's office one afternoon, my eyes were drawn to the cover of one of his marketing magazines. It showed a picture of a handsome executive and the bold headlines above the picture proclaimed, "AMA Chicago Chapter Names McDonald's Kroc Marketing Man of 1972."

"Who's Kroc?" I asked.

My friend, Nort Beckerman, looked at me in surprise and then told me. I was flabbergasted to learn that this man had parlayed a mundane thing like a hamburger into a $700 million chain of fast food restaurants.

I had never even eaten in one of his restaurants. Peggy and I had our favorite restaurants and dined out frequently, but our choice never included fast food. Perhaps living in Michigan, instead of Illinois, partially accounted for my ignorance. However, one thing occurred to me. If anyone should be able to tell me how to take a concept from the drawing board to reality, this had to be the man!

I took the magazine back to my house and read the article on Ray Kroc several times.

"What the hell," I thought. "What have I got to lose by asking?"

I sat down at a typewriter and began typing, "Dear Mr. Kroc . . ." On a single sheet of paper, without actually revealing what my concept was, I told Ray Kroc a little bit about my personal history and a lot about my problem of obtaining venture capital for a unique and worthwhile concept. I closed by asking for just twenty minutes of his time to get his opinions.

I all but forgot about the letter until I was summoned to the telephone two weeks later.

I took the receiver and answered, "Leeds."

The other voice came across clear and crisp, "Bob, this is Ray. How can I help you?"

I stopped and tried to think of who I might know by the name of Ray. I drew a blank.

49

After an embarrassing pause, the voice began again. "I'm Ray Kroc."

I still couldn't place the name.

"I'm Ray Kroc, from McDonald's!"

"Jesus Christ," I said to myself. "It's him! It's the guy from McDonald's hamburgers!"

Within a few minutes, the tone of Mr. Kroc's voice had me at ease, and his apparent sincerity and interest in my problems was confirmed by an appointment to meet with him at McDonald's Oakbrook headquarters the following week. It was to be one of the longest waits of my life.

The appearance of the eight-story McDonald's home office was intimidating, but the impression of the man who made this enterprise happen was nothing less than overwhelming.

His office was laid out similarly to all the offices on the eighth floor. It was a very contemporary arrangement with wide open areas and no permanent interior walls. The work area of each employee, from the chairman on down, was at least partially exposed to all the other employees. Only informal, moveable partitions gave a loose definition of each individual's work area.

By being tucked away in the far corner of the floor, Kroc's office was at least partially secluded. There were few executive trappings of the type one might expect to find in the office of a man who headed a multimillion dollar enterprise.

He appeared much older than the magazine picture I had seen, but his actions and exuberance were those of a young man. His handshake was warm and friendly. His greeting put me immediately at ease.

After a brief exchange of trivia, he invited me to reveal my mysterious concept to him. I started to open my charts on a nearby table, but with a wave of his hand he insisted that I place everything on his own desk. Nothing he could have done would have made me feel more comfortable.

I pointed to the artist's rendering of the buildings. "This is a pet motel, Mr. Kroc. It's a facility specifically designed for the boarding of pets when a pet owner goes on vacation."

A big smile spread across his face. "A pet motel?"

"A pet motel!" I said emphatically. "Mr. Kroc, there are over twenty-six million dogs and twenty-one million cats in American households today. But, in addition to these, there are another fourteen million other types of animals being kept as household pets. Up until now, no one has designed, built, and operated a facility that would deal with all the inherent problems of all-pet boarding."

As I talked on, his eyes kept wandering back to the artist's renderings. The smile never left his face, nor did he once interrupt me. When I was through, there was only a brief pause.

Kroc looked around at all the charts and documents covering his desk. "How much will all this cost?" he asked, still smiling.

"Land, sixty thousand. Buildings, two hundred, sixty-nine thousand, five hundred. Equipment, twenty-nine thousand, five hundred. Nonvariable, nonrecurring start-up expenses, fourteen thousand, six hundred dollars. A total of three hundred seventy-three thousand, six hundred dollars."

He began shaking his head from side to side. Finally, he said, "This is the goddamnedest thing I've seen since I thought of McDonald's!" He turned his head toward the front office and called out.

"Fred? Fred, come here for a minute."

A tall, good-looking man appeared from the other side of the partition.

"Fred, this is Robert Leeds." Fred Turner, the man Ray Kroc had plucked from behind a grill in a McDonald's restaurant and hand-groomed to succeed him, acknowledged the introduction with an abrupt nod of his head. Then, almost emotionless, his eyes darted to the renderings and the mass of statistics on Kroc's desk as Kroc explained my concept to him. There was an awkward silence when he had finished.

It was obvious to me that Turner wasn't impressed. I felt a little embarrassed, wondering how many times Kroc invited people like me to his office for similar shows. Turner simply nodded his head and disappeared back behind the partition. I felt it was an awkward moment, but if it was, Kroc didn't seem to notice.

"Have you got any plans for lunch?"

Before I could answer, he took me by the arm and we were heading toward the elevators.

We entered the unpretentious first-floor restaurant and were immediately seated by the manager. Within a few minutes, several McDonald's executives joined us. I was disappointed that the menu did not list any McDonald's fare. Here I was, sitting next to the man who had made the Big Mac a phenomenon, and I had never seen or tasted one. I settled for a bacon, lettuce, and tomato sandwich.

Kroc began by telling me he was a self-made man and then went on to tell me the story of how he had started McDonald's. Like so many others, his climb to the top was not without trials and adversities. It began when he was a partner in a company that had the rights to the multi-spindled malted milk shake mixers.

He recounted how he stood in a small California fast food restaurant and was fascinated to see hundreds of people lining up to buy identically prepared meals of hamburgers and french fries. He had just sold the McDonald brothers their second five-spindle milk shake machine, and they still couldn't keep up with the demand.

Ray became obsessed with buying out the McDonald brothers, but he could not raise the necessary money to do so. Although the exclusive sales rights to the multi-spindle mixing machines promised to be worth a lot of money, as a last resort he approached his partner and long-time friend to buy him out. Recognizing that Ray had no alternative, his partner made him a ridiculous offer. It was only a fraction of what Ray felt his interest was worth.

Ray accepted the offer, but not without the promise that he would some day get even. He was smiling, but his message was serious. "I don't get mad, I get even!"

In later years, his former partner became the president of one of America's largest paper products companies, and although McDonald's was using millions of dollars worth of paper dishes, cups, and napkins, not one penny's worth was bought from that company. Not until the man was dead did Kroc lift the ban, even though it had often meant paying a little more to someone else.

There was a message in his story, and I didn't miss the point.

When we returned to his office, Kroc straightened out my papers on his desk. He looked again at the artist's renderings of the buildings, and the broad smile returned to his face.

"I'd like you to leave these with me for a few days. O.K.?"

"Certainly," I agreed.

Shortly after, I was on my way back home. I thought about how many times before I had been full of hope and confidence. The feeling was different this time, but I had mixed emotions. I felt Kroc's genuine interest and appreciation of the concept, but, on the other hand, I was uncertain of just how he could really help me.

It would be a serious mistake for McDonald's to invest in a pet-boarding venture. I could imagine all the jokes and innuendos that would arise from such an association. On the other hand, Kroc had many friends. Many wealthy friends. His personal interest could be the ingredient necessary to put the investment package together.

# 7

# AN OFFER I
# COULDN'T REFUSE

The next several days were pure torture. I waited impatiently for some word to arrive. I wanted something to happen, but at the same time I remained skeptical that my meeting with Kroc would actually lead to anything.

I spent the next week typing out résumés. If I was going to keep trying, I was going to have to get some kind of job and get some money coming in.

Just when my spirits were flagging, I received a telephone call from Kroc's secretary. Mr. Kroc wanted me to meet with his attorneys at their office in Chicago. Things suddenly began looking up. Perhaps McDonald's was interested after all.

The law offices of Sonnenschein, Levinson, Carlin, Nath & Rosenthal occupied an entire floor of 69 West Washington Street. On their stationery were listed the names of ninety-seven active members of the firm. In addition to handling the legal matters for some of the largest companies in America, including McDonald's, at least two members of the law firm also represented the personal interests of McDonald's founder, Ray Kroc. I was impressed.

When we had finished the introductions, one of the lawyers paused and looked directly into my eyes.

"Mr. Leeds, McDonald's doesn't want to get involved with your pet motel . . . . However, Mr. Kroc would like to become involved personally."

I took a deep breath.

"Would you be interested in this arrangement?"

"Certainly!" I replied. It was far more than I had hoped.

"All right, let's go over to the club and discuss it over lunch."

The club turned out to be the Chicago Athletic Club on Michigan Avenue. When we were seated, and a round of drinks was served, one of the lawyers began.

"Mr. Leeds, you may be a very lucky man. Ray likes you and he thinks you have a terrific idea. He wants to help you himself. Now, you tell me what you want in order for him to become involved."

"Well," I replied slowly. "I need equity capital. I think I have investors with half the required three hundred seventy-five thousand dollars . . ."

Before I could finish, one of the lawyers cut me off. "No!" he said emphatically. "If Ray gets involved, there can't be any other investors. He's got to do the whole thing by himself. He doesn't need any other investors. He doesn't even need a bank. If he does this thing, he'll do it all by himself."

I thought for a while. Although I had several interested prospects, I hadn't made any commitments to any of them. There could be a lot of advantages to a single investor with Mr. Kroc's stature. I failed to see the potential hazards of such an arrangement.

Finally, I spoke up. "If it's investment capital, I don't see any problem. The one thing I don't want is a hundred percent debt capital. The interest payments would eat me up alive." They nodded in understanding.

"Good," the lawyer said. "Ray's worth six hundred and eighty-five million dollars. He doesn't need anyone else's money."

There was one other condition I wanted. It was the one thing I had held out for from the beginning. "I also want fifty-one percent of the stock. We can structure the company so Mr. Kroc's investment is protected, but I want to be able to control the company's operations." I wanted to be sure that the pet motel was never turned into another dog kennel.

The lawyers were shaking their heads from side to side.

"That's not possible, Mr. Leeds. You have to understand that a person in Mr. Kroc's position has certain obligations due to his tax requirements and also because of his arrangements with McDonald's. There's no way Mr. Kroc could participate in any venture unless he owned controlling interest."

I didn't understand what those requirements could be, but I had no reason then to believe it wasn't so. Both lawyers began assuring me that I was about to become one of the luckiest persons in the world, and my reluctance started to weaken.

"If you go along with Mr. Kroc, you could be a millionaire in five years. Maybe a multimillionaire."

Then came a succession of stories about people who had cast their lot with Kroc, stories about people who had trusted Ray when he started out and who were now worth millions. To hear them tell it, no one had ever been disappointed. Not only was he a man of unquestionable integrity, but he was one of those rare individuals who rewarded his associates generously. He never forgot favors and he never forgot his friends. But, they hastened to add, he also never forgot those who crossed him or took advantage of him.

Together, the lawyers spelled out the terms of what they thought was a fair arrangement and one that might be acceptable to Kroc. Mr. Kroc would put up the money to build the three pet motels planned for the Chicago area. We would build only one pet motel in the beginning, and if the concept proved economically feasible, we would build the other two. No bank monies would be used. Ray could do all the financing necessary. I would be president and have total operating control. Kroc's wife, Joan, would be vice president and would become actively involved in the company because of her interest in animal welfare.

The fact that Mr. Kroc had over $685 million to back the growth of the company kept coming up over and over again in their conversation. If it was meant to influence me, it did.

In exchange for putting up all the money, Ray would retain title to the land and buildings and take all the depreciation. After the company was financially sound, it would buy the land and buildings from the Krocs at a price we would negotiate at the time. I thought I

56

knew what that meant, and I didn't object. Anyone who stood the initial risk deserved to make a good profit on his investment. The proposal sounded perfectly fair, up to that point.

The last part of the proposal was not the least by far. Of the one thousand shares of stock to be issued, Ray would own 85 percent and I would own 15 percent.

Fifteen percent! The words came as a shock.

Perhaps if I had been worldly wise, I would not have been surprised. Venture capital has a price few speculators would even imagine. The best idea in the world isn't worth a plug nickel if it isn't brought into being. My rounds of the venture capital companies should have prepared me for this kind of demand. I used to teach my graduate business students the same thing. Now it was time to test my own preachments.

My sense of disappointment must have been apparent to everyone. Once again the lawyers began telling me how fortunate I could be if I accepted Mr. Kroc's offer.

"What's the difference if you own fifteen percent or ninety-nine percent as long as you wind up with several million dollars in a few years? Look at it this way. Is it better to have fifteen percent of something, or one hundred percent of nothing?"

It was an old and tired cliche that I had heard a million times. But it was true.

One of the lawyers began again, and the offer took on a more positive glow.

"We'll start you out at twenty-five thousand dollars a year and, of course, your expenses. You'll get a company car, a health insurance program, and all the regular perks. If it will make you feel better, we'll also give you a five-year employment contract. That should be plenty of time for you to prove yourself."

When he had finished, the whole deal didn't sound bad at all. Maybe it was the content. Maybe it was the martinis.

"O.K." I said. "We've got a deal."

"Well, wait," one of the lawyers cautioned. "We can only recommend these terms to Ray, but it's up to him to accept them."

I doubted that, but I let it pass. I finished another martini but barely disturbed my food. For the balance of the meal I listened to them tell me how lucky I was and how rich I was about to become. I listened and I loved it.

I lived the next week in ecstasy and agony. Ecstasy at the prospect of becoming Ray Kroc's partner in the pet-motel business, and agony at hearing Peggy upbraid me for agreeing to give away controlling interest in the dream that we had sacrificed so much for. Despite all my assurances that we could be millionaires in five years, she refused to be swayed. The eighth wonder of the world: A wife's intuition.

I had an attorney review the contracts to make sure all the important items were covered and our interests properly protected. At first he flinched when I told him I was giving Kroc 85 percent of the stock in exchange for putting up the construction money. However, after hearing me recite the history of my capital-seeking exploits, he reflected that a bird in the hand was worth two in the bush.

The following week, in the Krocs' Lake Shore Drive mansion, amidst cocktails and hors d'oeuvres, Peggy looked on as I signed the contracts that made me a partner with one of the world's richest men. Joining us in the festive occasion was one of the Krocs' lawyers and Burgy, the Krocs' miniature schnauzer.

For me it was the culmination of a long struggle, long sieges of hopelessness and brief periods of misguided elation. It had been years of real dreams and false beginnings. In that single evening, Ray Kroc and his lovely wife, Joan, made it all worthwhile.

His attorneys had not misled me. Again and again, Ray and Joan told us how enthusiastic they were about the whole concept for improving pet care in America. Watching the way Ray picked up and fondled his dog only fortified the instinctive feeling that I had about the man. It was a truly joyous occasion for all. Perhaps only one of many for the Krocs, but a singular moment in my lifetime.

At the end of the evening, we were treated to another example of Ray's generosity. As we were getting ready to leave, I brought up the subject of the company car. I told him that I had always driven a Cadillac and if there were no objections, I would like to have one as a company car. I started to tell him that the difference between leasing a Cadillac and a Chevrolet would be paid for out of my salary, but before I could get the words out, Ray raised his voice.

"Hey. Listen here. We're going to make a lot of money together. You want a Cadillac? Get a Cadillac! You're president of the company, you do any god-damned thing you want!"

I could feel the shudders run up and down his lawyer's spine. (I got my Cadillac but I always paid the difference between its cost and that of a Chevrolet out of my own pocket.)

In the quiet of the hallway, I swept Peggy into my arms and hugged her. "Well, was I right?"

Although her eyes were sparkling, and she stood there holding me tightly, she whispered, "Remember, I don't trust anybody!"

I dismissed her pessimism as a typical feminine characteristic. In a few years, I would call her prophetic and wish I had heeded her instincts. It would be the last time I would ever accept the adage that a bird in the hand was worth two in the bush without knowing what kind of bird I would be holding.

When we arrived home, we sat down and reflected on how far we had come since I had brought Peggy to America from Finland. We literally started with nothing and even had to borrow money to get from New York to Detroit. Jobs were so scarce that our salvation lay in my ability to get into college on the G.I. Bill.

We had taken a cigar box and divided the inside area into twelve small spaces. Each month, I would cash my government check for rolls of coins, and together, like a ritual, we would sit down together and divide the change among the different compartments. Rent, electricity, water, coal, food, medical, insurance, clothing, entertainment, and miscellaneous.

Somehow, the money always ran out before we got to the entertainment compartment. More often than not, one crisis or another required more than we had budgeted and Peggy reluctantly took the additional amount from the space marked "food."

Odd jobs and hand-me-downs scarcely carried us from one crisis to another. Being able to sell a pint of my rare O-negative blood to the local blood bank every eight weeks was something we counted on to make it through the year. From time to time, when my mother wasn't looking, my father would slip a dollar bill into my hand and whisper to me to take Peggy to a movie show. It was a luxury he rarely, if ever, bestowed upon himself.

If I was now cautious about spending money, it was a reflex conditioned by a lifetime of experience. Being partners with a free-spending, multimillionaire would be a new experience and one that I would have to get used to.

When Ray called and suggested that I interview the McDonald's architect for the job of designing our first pet motel, I knew better than to refuse. Although my own architect had completed the preliminary designs, the least I could do was talk to Ray's friend.

I readily understood why this young man enjoyed such popularity with Ray. Not only did he impress me as being personable and highly qualified, but he radiated the kind of enthusiasm I enjoyed associating with.

Taking up a pad and a pencil, the young man began sketching exterior wall treatments and building shapes that added whole new dimensions to the concept. His talent and Ray's subtle coercion convinced me to give him the job of designing our first pet motel.

I turned over all my preliminary plans together with the recommendations of the National Academy of Sciences-National Research Council. By following these recommendations, we could build the finest commercial pet-care center in the world.

There were two additional considerations I insisted he agree to. Every year, I read about some animal facility burning down with tragic loss of animal life. I never wanted to be faced with that possibility. All of our animal facilities would have to be constructed to meet local fire resistant code requirements.

I emphasized the second requirement several times to be sure he understood its importance. "Remember," I admonished him, "it's got to be built for under three hundred and seventy-five thousand dollars!"

"I don't see any problem with that figure," he said, smiling. "Trust me!"

# 8

# IT'S ONLY MONEY

Although Ray offered the services of McDonald's staff, I learned very early that it would be to my best interest to proceed on my own. My first lesson was a letter to Ray from McDonald's Vice President of Corporate Real Estate. In a two-page departmental communication, the man listed several reasons why my projection of land costs was unrealistic and predicted we would spend twice what I had allocated. A short time later, I acquired a beautiful eight-and-a-half acre site in the northwest Chicago suburb of Prairie View. The total cost was 30 percent below my estimate.

With each contact, I came to realize that the McDonald's people were spoiled by their financial success. Their company was making a lot of money, and they could spend a lot of money.

It became apparent to me from the very beginning that the budget of $375,000 would not be met unless I monitored every facet of the design and the construction.

Despite the architect's denials, when I looked at the blueprints, I could tell that the construction cost would be double or even triple our original budget. Neither my dedication to fiscal responsibility nor my increased warnings that the architect was the wrong man for the job received a sympathetic response from Ray. Each time I called him to complain, Ray would launch into a tirade and order me to let the architect do his work.

Finally, after several months of frustration, Peggy and I were summoned to a luncheon meeting with Joan Kroc. We met at the plush Tavern Club, a private restaurant in downtown Chicago.

Joan was waiting for us at her table, looking like she had just stepped out of a fashion magazine. She was much younger than Ray and extremely attractive. It was easy to understand why Ray was so proud of her.

She greeted us warmly and ordered each of us our choice of drinks. We talked about the pet motel and our progress, or lack of it. I knew she was familiar with some of the problems.

She listened patiently while I tried to emphasize that the profitability of the new company depended on our holding the building cost to our original budget. I explained that the only way to prove whether or not the concept was viable was to build it the way we originally planned and then see what kind of profit we could generate.

The same sympathetic smile was on her face when I finished. "Listen to me, Robert. Ray and I don't care if the company never makes a profit. We both think the idea is just great. We love it. Don't even worry about making a profit." Her eyes never left mine and she emphasized the right words to make sure I understood what she meant.

"Ray and I are worth six hundred and eighty-five million dollars, and we'll never live long enough to spend it all. We don't care how much the buildings cost. We don't care if the company ever makes a profit. We're not doing this for the money. We're doing it for you and Peggy. Ray wants to make you rich, and if you stop fighting him, he will. So what if the architect does go over the budget? It doesn't matter. Ray wants the first motel to be a showplace. Do it right! You can build the second one within your budget and prove the economics then. The money isn't important. Believe me!"

I understood what she was saying, but instinctively, I felt she was wrong. The money *did* count. Their accountant let me know it every time he paid a bill. It would be a monumental embarrassment to me to spend a million dollars on something I said could be built for under $375,000. More important was the indifference to a return on the investment.

I was counting on my 15 percent of the profits. That

15 percent was important to me, and if there were no profits, Peggy and I would be the ones who would do without. I was reluctant to say this to Joan, though. I felt that if I did, she would go back to Ray, and he would just increase my wages. I didn't want charity, I wanted to prove the concept on its own. I wanted to earn my money the old-fashioned way.

"I'll tell you what we'll do," Joan said. "We'll figure the return on investment based on your budget figure and not on how much is actually spent. That way, everyone will have what he wants."

All my major objections were quashed. I didn't ask her to confirm it in writing. Certainly that would have been presumptuous. Joan Kroc was a lady and naive gentlemen don't ask ladies to reduce their word to writing.

Joan held her glass up to toast the arrangement, and I lifted mine to hers. Suddenly, my glass slipped from my grasp and fell to the table, spilling its contents down the front of her dress.

I was mortified. Before I could move, Joan blotted the excess moisture with her napkin and ordered each of us a fresh drink. The waiter directed us to a clean table, and she continued talking as if nothing had happened.

When we parted, we agreed that I would not question anything the architect did and I would not bother Ray about such frivolous concerns as cost overruns. In exchange, the profitability of the pet motel would be based on an investment of $375,000, regardless of how much Ray spent.

Over the next several months, I watched as earlier construction mistakes resulted in more costly remedial efforts. Foundations had been poured in the wrong places, and now certain prefabricated equipment could not be accommodated. Major electrical terminals could not be found and had to be rerun through the ceilings. Heating duct space was almost nonexistent, and the ducting had to be bent and twisted to be installed. Lobby walls were built, torn down, and then rebuilt to mask the results of ineptness. Even the manager's residence wasn't exempt. When the refrigerator arrived, the kitchen counters were too long to permit opening its door. And with each new effort the construction costs soared.

It was obvious we were way over budget, but I kept to my word and stayed away from Ray. By the middle of June 1972, construction costs exceeded one million dollars, and Ray Kroc never voiced a single word of complaint. In fact, he seemed to take pride in how much the facility was costing.

Shortly before the scheduled date of our grand opening, Ray called me with another offer I couldn't refuse. A lady who operated a nonprofit animal shelter had been asking him to donate some money to it. Ray explained that he'd like to give the woman five or ten thousand dollars, but thought that a good way to do it would be through American Pet Motels. That way, the woman would get the benefit of the money and we would get the benefit of the favorable publicity. Ray had already talked to his public relations firm and they had some good ideas to discuss with me.

The lady was Gertrude Maxwell, a retired schoolteacher who had dedicated her life to rescuing abandoned pets. What made her Save-A-Pet Animal Foundation unique was that she took in stray and abandoned pets and would never let one be euthanized. If it was sick, she had a veterinarian heal it. Regardless of the pet's age or condition, if she couldn't find someone to adopt it, Gertrude kept the animal at her decrepit shelter, where it was fed and cared for. It was a formidable challenge for a compassionate senior citizen already approaching her seventies. I welcomed the opportunity to help.

When construction continued to lag, Joan interceded and got the architect to commit himself to a June 23 completion date. Our grand opening was scheduled accordingly.

As a commercial pet-boarding facility, our motel's appearance was a marvel. A brilliant red roof highlighted the low gray buildings. When you stepped through the double glass doors into the lobby, you had to remind yourself that you were not entering a first-class luxury hotel. The simulation was excellent. The architect's minor oversight of not providing space for the reception desk had to be worked out by deleting two feet of space in the entrance area. However, only those customers who have gotten caught in the swinging entrance doors have had any adverse comments about this adjustment.

The problem of obtaining mattresses for our miniature brass beds was resolved with a single telephone call to the local Sealy Mattress Company and an explanation of what the mattresses were needed for. A week before we opened, our driver pulled up to the Sealy loading dock and picked up a truckload of specially constructed two-inch-thick foam rubber, waterproof mattresses. For our canine guests, sleeping at the pet motel would be "like sleeping on a cloud."

The grand opening was a memorable black-tie affair. A huge pink-and-white-striped circus tent was set up on our front acreage, and an orchestra played popular melodies while guests glided to and fro on the specially installed dance floor. A huge buffet offered all kinds of delicacies, and uniformed waitresses darted from table to table to oblige the guests' special wishes. At each corner of the tent, a bar had been set up to provide liquid refreshments.

Except for our neighbors, each guest was required to purchase a ticket, and all the proceeds were given to the Save-A-Pet Animal Foundation. Guided tours of the pet motel's different accommodations were conducted by our employees, in their smart red, white, and blue animal attendant uniforms.

Ray and Joan attended and joined in the festivities. I was embarrassed to find that Ray only drank one brand of bourbon, and it was one we had neglected to have available. One of the employees made a hasty trip to a nearby liquor store.

The Krocs didn't show up alone. In his arms, Ray carried their little schnauzer, Burgy. Wearing a white dress collar with a black bow tie, the dog was as formally attired as any of the guests.

I didn't mention to Ray that only thirty-four of the two hundred and sixty-eight dog runs were usable, or that one hundred and eighty kennel gates, built according to the architect's plans, were inoperable. No one noticed that the quick disconnects for the sanitizing hoses had been anchored flush with the concrete, making them unusable, or that all of the electrical outlets in the kennels had been covered by the fencing posts so they were completely inaccessible.

All problems were set aside, and I had no intention of bringing anything up that might cast a pall on the day's festivities. This was a day to let my partner savor the potential of our aspirations, and I would let him do so without recrimination. He was delighted with what he saw, and I let him depart with those feelings.

The following day, the entire process was to be repeated for the members of Chicago's veterinary profession. This was a most important occasion because we anticipated a large part of our business to come from veterinary referrals.

To our dismay, the swarm of veterinarians failed to appear. The band played to an empty house, and heaping trays of food went uneaten. By the end of the day, only a handful of veterinarians had made an appearance, and none of them could explain why others failed to show up.

It wasn't until Monday that I understood. Apparently, someone at McDonald's public relations firm had forgotten to mail the invitations and remembered them only the day before the event. Less than a dozen received the invitation on Saturday. The rest received theirs the next week.

# 9

# THE GUESTS ARRIVE

The following Monday, June 25, 1973, American Pet Motels was opened to the public.

To say that we were overwhelmed would be the understatement of the year. Not only from the Chicago area, but from as far away as Michigan, Indiana, and Wisconsin, people brought their pets to a facility that, for the first time, offered them the safety, security, and care they sought.

There was one problem. With only forty-two of our dog runs usable, we occupied our time inventing reasons for declining business. Not until after the peak boarding season had passed would most of the facilities be suitable for use. In appearance, our operation was a huge success. Financially, it was a disaster. A kennel makes most of its money during the summer months, and this was the period we missed.

The construction repairs continued for several more months, and as more accommodations became available, we readily filled them with the potential clientele I had predicted.

Dogs, cats, rabbits, horses, goats, mice, olingos, coatimundis, foxes, wolves, raccoons, squirrels, ducks, mink, fish, ferrets, birds, snakes, lizards, skunks, monkeys, apes—you name it, and we boarded it. It was only a short time before we lived up to our slogan, "If it walks, creeps, crawls, flies, swims, slithers, or hops, we will board it." We did!

There were conditions under which we would refuse a pet. We would not board a vicious or poisonous pet, nor one with a contagious illness. In addition, each owner had to show written proof that the pet's vaccinations were up to date. We would not expose either our employees or other people's pets to these hazards.

From the beginning, I began to realize how provincial many pet owners are in their attitude toward other types of pets. The most compassionate dog owner may abhor cats, while a doting cat owner fails to find any virtue in owning a dog.

Perhaps pet owners should be classified by the species of pet they own. I have seen people spend more money on the care of a common house rat than they would feel justified in spending for another person's dog or cat. Many even fail to feel any common emotion for any form of pet except their own.

An example of this attitude occurred while I was at the front desk one day. A woman who had just paid a boarding bill of over $200 for a plain old nondescript cat was waiting for her pet to be brought to her. As the attendant placed the undistinguished feline on the counter, a man standing nearby, waiting to check in his dog, took one look at the cat and blurted out, "Why would you pay two hundred and fifteen dollars to board a cat like that? You could have gotten another one for less than five dollars!"

I almost laughed out loud, but the look in the lady's eyes warned me not to. She gazed at the man as if she couldn't believe what she had heard. Her lips quivered, but she repressed whatever she wanted to say. Instead, she clutched her cat close to her and stormed out of the building. This same man then boarded his mangy mongrel in our finest and most expensive suite. The value of a pet lies in the heart of the owner.

Such an attitude was responsible for one of my most trying experiences with a dog owner. The woman suddenly realized we also boarded reptiles and, apparently, she did not consider eight acres of space with carefully constructed security areas adequate protection for her dog. I showed her the security tanks with their locking lids and the solid door that stood between the serpentarium and the rest of the buildings, but nothing would assuage her concerns. Before she finally agreed to leave her pet, I had to guarantee that no attendant who

68

touched a snake would ever feed or touch her dog. I doubt that she enjoyed her trip knowing that somewhere within our boundaries there might be a harmless snake, even though the snake would undoubtedly be more afraid of her dog than her dog would be of it.

Snakes are more common pets than most people presume and are owned for a variety of reasons. For children and many adults, it appears to be a mixture of curiosity and fascination. For one of my enterprising clients, the reason was strictly business.

I recall coming in one day and seeing a huge boa constrictor in the monkey cage. It had been placed there because no aquarium tank we had was large enough to hold it comfortably. As I was watching, a buxom young lady entered the room with our attendant and began rearranging the cage. The lady's male companion proudly informed me that she was the "famous" exotic dancer who had been performing in a local all-nude cabaret show, and his wife.

"When we get back, you gotta come over and see her do her snake dance. Just ask for me and I'll get you in free," he invited.

"Thanks a lot," I said. I smiled as a picture came into my mind of Peggy tying the snake in a knot around my neck if she ever found out I visited a place like that for any reason.

On another occasion, I received a telephone call from a public relations man at the Palmer House Hotel in downtown Chicago. The opera star, Patrice Munsel, was staying at the hotel and was traveling, as she always did, with her pet boa constrictor.

The agent thought it would be a good publicity gimmick if we sent our pet limousine, a specially equipped twenty-eight-foot Travco mobile van, to the Palmer House, and Ms. Munsel permitted the press to photograph her sending her pet boa to the pet motel.

In situations like this, we usually agree to participate because the publicity is as good for us as it is for the other party. However, at the last minute the plans were cancelled. Apparently, Ms. Munsel objected to parting with the snake for even a short time. She cared much more for her pet boa than she did for any publicity the story might generate.

Although we have now boarded hundreds of snakes, the question of whether we will continue to do so remains up in the air. With few exceptions, snakes will not eat anything unless it is alive. In my own mind, I find the thought of feeding one live animal to another a contradiction of the philosophy I practice. I know about the laws of nature and the different requirements of balance that exist, and I can abide with it in nature where it occurs without my participation. But in my own animal shelters, I consider the taking of any kind of animal life an impugning of my beliefs. While many people may not agree, I am sure that those who have raised common field mice and alley rats as affectionate, trained pets would concur.

I suppose we all share some ambivalent attitudes toward different forms of life, and I am no exception. Although I loathe poisonous snakes and many insects, Peggy would be the first to confirm that I harbor strange respect for some lesser life forms. I will not harm a cricket or beetle that has found its way into our home. To her everlasting consternation, I absolutely forbid harming or even disturbing some little spiders (and some pretty big ones also) who have decided to share our home. When we lived in the south, disagreements over spiders became an increasingly familiar occurrence. If you've never lived in Florida, you can't even imagine what I mean.

The longer I was in the business, the more I began to worry that my attitude might be reaching the borderline of senile benevolence. Fortunately, the more people I met, the more I realized that although we are a minority, we are many.

My confidence received a major boost when I met the new general manager of the Kasco Dog Food Company. It was a warm spring morning, just after a long period of rain, and the walkway to the pet motel was littered with floundering earthworms.

As I stepped from my car, this man introduced himself, and I invited him in to discuss his line of foods. I began walking toward the front doors, being very careful not to step on any of the worms littering the path. As I reached the lobby door, I suddenly realized that I was alone. I turned around and, to my surprise, I saw

70

this well-dressed stranger picking up earthworms and depositing them in the safety of the nearby grass. It was an act of consideration that pleased me immensely, and I promptly joined him until the very last worm disappeared into the safety of the tall grass.

At the time, I thought that we were probably the only two people in the world crazy enough to do such a thing. Since then, I have met many who perform the same ritual. Guardians of the lowly worm. I like to think the good Lord looks kindly upon such acts.

Many people, regardless of their lot in life, devote a disproportionate share of their time, effort, and money to aiding injured wildlife, and one of the pleasures of my business has been to meet many of them.

Only recently, a man drove up to our entrance just as Marc was unlocking the front doors. Holding a brown paper bag in one hand, he stepped out of his Mercedes 560SEC and approached Marc. The man explained that he had been driving to work when a sparrow struck his windshield and fell onto the roadway. Rather than leave the bird lying there, he had pulled his car onto the shoulder and got out to move its body off the road. However, upon picking up the bird, he found that it was still alive and so decided to bring it to us for veterinary care. When Marc explained that we only boarded animals, the man requested that we have one of our visiting veterinarians treat the bird and that we board it until it was well enough to return to the wild. He offered to leave a large enough deposit to cover all the costs.

A few hours later, the bird was alert and walking around its cage, and by that evening it was flying as well as it ever had. I took the cage outside and watched the little bird fly off into the sunset. It was a pleasure to return the man's deposit along with a little note thanking him for his concern for our feathered friends.

On another occasion, an elderly, retired couple brought in a squirrel that had been injured by a BB pellet. They had paid a veterinarian to treat the wound, but now they were going to visit their children on the Coast and needed a safe place where the squirrel could recuperate. The squirrel was with us for almost two months before the couple returned to claim it. They gratefully paid the boarding bill of over fifty dollars and took off for the Wisconsin border, where the dense woods and lack of human habitation offered the animal the safety the old couple sought for it.

Each succeeding day, the elderly couple climbed into their old Chevrolet and drove the thirty-five miles just to check on the squirrel's well-being. The first couple of days, the squirrel came down from the tree and accepted food from them, but on the third day it stood perched on its limb and only watched. From then on, it never came to them again, but the old lady assured me she could hear the chattering of another squirrel nearby and was convinced her squirrel had found a mate. I'd like to think so.

I suspect there are more individuals secretly operating private animal shelters than we could ever imagine, and I can't think of a better way to spend one's retirement.

One of the strangest house pets ever boarded at the pet motel was a six-foot-long iguana. It was so long that we had to procure a bathtub in which to contain it. It wasn't only ugly, it was downright mean and disrespectful. When it wanted to show its displeasure, the iguana would lurch its body sideways and spit a bolt of black substance across the eight-foot room at its target. I was never so glad to have a guest leave as I was this one.

Not too many months later, another iguana was boarded with us. It was the same size but had a totally different disposition. It arrived in a limousine and was led in with a harness and leash by a uniformed chauffeur.

"If you let anything happen to Peter Pan here, the lady will kill you," he warned.

This iguana loved attention and especially enjoyed having his stomach rubbed. Never did he exhibit the barbarous demeanor of our earlier guest.

One of our regular guests was a fifty-two-year-old Greek land turtle owned by the wife of the German consul in Chicago. She had found it many years before and had adopted it as a pet. When they were being transferred to Washington, they brought the turtle in for boarding and for later shipment to their new location. I remember watching the woman break down and cry because she was worried the turtle might not survive the trip, but he did just fine.

Many strange people and animals have come through our front doors. There was the time a very well-dressed lady in a full-length mink coat came in leading a goat. It seems that her husband, having forgotten their wedding anniversary, had slipped out of the house and driven to the nearby shopping center in her brand-new Lincoln. Unable to decide what to buy her, he went into an establishment that offered alcoholic beverages and comaraderie. Fortunately, or unfortunately, the gentleman who occupied the next seat turned out to be the owner of a traveling petting zoo, and he offered the husband a solution to his quest. The more the husband drank, the better the option sounded, and in the end, he loaded this rare Nubian goat and two prize Peruvian roosters into the back seat of the Lincoln and returned home.

"Can you imagine?" the lady asked with a grin. "He brought this smelly goat home on the back seat of my brand-new Lincoln." That seemed the only thing that perturbed her.

The goat boarded with us for several days until the couple had a special fence erected to protect it from their dogs. The episode reminded me of the time I brought Peggy the coatimundi for an anniversary gift, and she cried for two days.

Some of our other exotic guests have presented us with equally exotic challenges.

We thought we had every kind of cage, container, or room necessary to confine any type of pet. But we didn't then, and we don't now. And, I doubt if anyone ever will have. The cunning ability of certain members of the animal kingdom is beyond mere man's comprehension.

Proof of this was a pet raccoon named Rocky.

Rocky Raccoon loved to roam freely or cuddle in one of the attendant's laps. However, our attendants couldn't always be there to watch him, so he was frequently contained in a special heavy-duty five-foot-square monkey cage.

When I entered the pet motel one morning, I couldn't believe my eyes. The doors to Rocky's cage and room were wide open. Most of the store shelves were wiped clean of products, and most of the food products were opened and their remains strewn about the floor. Tucked away on a shelf behind the front desk, amidst all our motel forms, was our culprit, Rocky, sound asleep.

Sometime during the night, he had managed to unbolt the door hinges to his cage and escape. He must have had a royal time. He visited the aviary and other small animal rooms, scrounging for food but not disturbing any of the animals. Apparently, sampling the diets of other animals wasn't sufficient, so he decided to try the pet food that was stacked on shelves in our store. Rocky also consumed an entire bag of potato chips, part of a box of chocolate chip cookies, and several candy bars that the receptionists kept behind the counter.

Rocky was placed back in his cage, none the worse for his escapade, and additional restraints proved an adequate match for his efforts on subsequent visits.

Monkeys and apes presented similar problems. Simians seem to have a peculiar ability to perceive the slightest weakness in their confining structure. An ape will select the junction of two or more bars and by determined shaking and twisting, all too frequently will be able to pry them apart. In an orderly sequence, the ape will then proceed to take each adjoining link of the cage apart until there is a hole sufficiently large for it to exit through.

It is a miracle that we have never lost one of these precocious guests, but that is probably due to an ever-increasing vigilance and continued efforts to anticipate what could possibly happen next.

We learned another characteristic of monkeys the hard way. Because they attract a lot of attention, we like to board them in a room off the main lobby, where visitors can watch their silly antics. This particular room is decorated to give the appearance of a rain forest and includes several artificial trees.

The first time we boarded a monkey there, we made sure it could not reach the plants and damage them. What we failed to consider was that its tail had twice the span of its arms and could be just as destructive.

The following morning, we arrived to find the plants in thousands of little plastic sections, lying all over the floor. Experience can be an exasperating teacher.

# 10

# EMPLOYEES ARE SPECIAL PEOPLE

By our second year, 1974, we had twenty-six employees, an average of one person for every sixteen pets. Not only were we making money, but our boarding rates remained competitive with the other kennels in our area and, in fact, were lower than those many other kennels were charging to keep a pet in a cage.

Mass boarding was not only profitable, but it permitted a higher level of care than is possible in most smaller kennels.

Selective hiring had a great deal to do with our early success. I was never doubtful about our potential for success, but I was equally convinced that it could only be achieved if the staff recognized a specific order of responsibility. This led to the formulation of a set of priorities that we stressed to both management and employees. These priorities became our "Hierarchy of Obligations," and I expected every employee to know them and to abide by them.

Our first obligation was to the welfare of the animal. No matter what occurred, we expected an employee to attend to a pet's needs first. No attendant was to go to lunch or go home if one of his or her animals still required attention. If an animal wasn't eating well, we expected the employee to find something the pet would eat, even if it meant coming to me for something special. If it was necessary to stay after hours, we expected the employee to do so; we would pay for the time. The welfare of the animals was of paramount importance and the primary obligation of us all.

Our second obligation was to the pet owner. Many people cannot enjoy their vacations if they are worried about their pets. We expected our employees to be sympathetic and understanding so that every pet owner left the premises confident that we would provide his pet the best possible care.

The third obligation was a shared one. The employee's obligation to the company and the company's obligation to the employee were equal. Neither could be greater than the other's. For our part, we tried as hard as our limited resources permitted. A huge turkey for Christmas, an annual company dinner at one of the finest restaurants, paid vacations, medical insurance, and a tuition refund program to encourage continued education were all provided in addition to the benefits other small companies gave. All we asked our employees in return was that they take good care of our clients.

Except for those whose sole duty was exercising dogs, employees had to be mature and over sixteen years of age. In addition, each one was required to take a battery of tests from which a psychological profile was drawn. We were concerned about employing someone who might abuse or otherwise injure an animal.

We strictly enforced one rule. If a customer was told we would do something for their pet, it had to be done! Our first director of animal welfare was also the first casualty of this rule.

Charles was brought to APM from Hollywood, where he had operated a show kennel for a movie star. If vanity had an image, it was Charles. All day long, he would strut about the premises lamenting the fact that cruel, unknown forces had deprived him of his just role as a major Hollywood star. At the slightest pretext, he would open the album he usually carried with him and begin showing customers old newspaper clippings and pictures of him standing beside famous actors and actresses, most of whom had long since retired from the scene.

Shortly after he joined us, it became obvious that Charles was spending a disproportionate amount of his time on his past rather than on our future, and he was

77

not inclined to change even after several warnings.

One evening, I returned to the motel after the dogs had been locked in for the night and decided to inspect the kennels. As I suspected, there was evidence that a few of the dogs had been locked into rooms that were not clean. In addition, I couldn't find any trace of cookies in any of the rooms. I knew that most of the dogs devoured the Milk Bones we passed out each night, but there always was one or two who did not eat them.

I went to the director's quarters and asked Charles about the cookies.

"You mean you really expected me to give them cookies every night?"

I just stared at the man.

"Oh, I know you kept asking me about them and talking about the dogs' 'cookie breaks,' but I thought you were just saying those things for show. I didn't think you really meant it. The people don't have any way of knowing."

We had spent two hundred dollars to have him interviewed by one of Chicago's best employment psychologists before hiring him and had paid all his moving expenses from California. We had trained him and tutored him. Still, it was a lost cause. It was good-bye, Charles. We don't do anything just for show! He just had too much Hollywood in him.

Sometimes, when you do hire the wrong person, thanks to the malignant benevolence of modern labor relations laws, it takes a tragedy to resolve the situation. We've had our share of these.

One case involved a sweet young woman whom we soon began to suspect was using drugs. Several signs were apparent, but there was no hard evidence we could confront her with to justify discharging her. Unfortunately, some of the other employees knew she was getting high and had actually seen her go out in back of the kennels to smoke, but due to a warped sense of peer loyalty, they didn't want to turn her in.

One day, just at quitting time, this girl stopped on her way out of the building to report that one of her dogs was missing. We knew it had been there when we opened the kennels because the director of animal welfare had seen it in its room that morning. The girl could not remember if the dog had eaten its food that day or anything else about it.

A thorough search of the kennels and grounds failed to turn up the little dog. Escape was virtually impossible. The gates to its dog run were closed. There was an escape barrier over the top of the run. The entire kennel was enclosed in an additional six-foot-high chain link fence, and beyond that was another seven-foot-high fence with three rows of barbed wire. With dozens of employees and customers walking around the facilities all day long, it was just not possible for a dog to be running around loose without being seen.

The dog was never found. The girl was discharged but never revealed what occurred. Even the dog's owners interviewed the girl at her home, but she was as vague then as she was the day we discharged her.

This incident led to a policy of having regular drug searches conducted on our property by the National K-9 Security Company. All employees are aware that a handler with a trained drug-detecting dog checks all rooms and lockers on our premises. Anyone found with an illegal drug will be discharged immediately.

One of our policies requires any female employee who handles cats to terminate her employment immediately upon becoming pregnant. It is a fair, practical, and humane rule. Cats are the main carriers of toxoplasmosis, a disease that is readily transmitted to the fetus of pregnant women, and can cause a number of tragic birth defects. When we hire women, we explain the policy and the reason for it to them and make sure they understand this condition of employment.

As luck would have it, one of our best receptionists announced that she was pregnant. However, when we reminded her of our policy, she countered that Illinois law forbade the discharge of a female employee because of pregnancy. She further advised us that although her pediatrician had advised her to quit, she intended to work for as long as she was able.

I called the Illinois Department of Labor and they confirmed that despite the health risk involved, if we discharged the girl we would have to continue to pay her full salary until she was able to return to work.

They had no provision for the consequences of toxoplasmosis or a deformed baby.

The idea of drafting a release and having her sign it occurred to me, but both my own attorneys and the state's advised me that any agreement the mother signed would be useless because the state would bring an action on behalf of the baby.

It was a Catch-22. If we discharged her, we would have to replace her and still pay her a full salary while she sat at home. If we permitted her to continue working and she contracted toxoplasmosis, we would be sued if the baby was born with any birth defects.

A few weeks had passed when the woman walked into my office and announced that her pediatrician had insisted that she quit so this was to be her last day. We were relieved, but only temporarily. Sometime later, she visited the motel to advise us that she had tested positive for toxoplasmosis and wanted us to know about it. Fortunately for everyone, the baby was born in perfect health.

The employees who have not measured up have been exceptions. In the vast majority of cases over the years, I have had a great deal of admiration and respect for the men and women who work for us. Most people who like to work with animals are special. There are always those to whom it is just another job, but there are many more to whom it is a dedicated obligation. These are the ones who take their lunch into the room of some new dog who is not adjusting well and sit there sharing their sandwich with the animal.

I never cease to be amazed that after only a few days on the job, these employees can identify any one of the dogs in their kennel by sight or by their room number. They can tell you how much the pet ate the previous day and even the condition of its stool. These are the people who make a pet-care facility outstanding.

On a number of occasions, I have walked into a kennel and found balloons hanging from an animal's mailbox, a cupcake complete with a candle, and maybe even a chew bone or other treat, all provided by one of the employees who wanted to give the animal a birthday party. It's a pure joy to have this type of worker.

Although we have had some excellent male employees,

the majority of our animal attendants have been women. I often jest that we employ not only the best workers of any kennel, but the best-looking ones, also. I would like to believe that our supervisors do not let looks influence their decisions, but for some reason, we have had some terrifically endowed employees whose figures were only slightly enhanced by our red, white, and blue hot pants uniforms.

One of these was our grooming manager. Karen was about five feet tall with blond hair and a well-proportioned body. The lobby's glass wall permitted people to look on while Karen and the other groomers bathed and groomed their dogs.

One of her regular customers was a local resident who was probably in his seventies. At first, every eight weeks, and then every six weeks, the man would walk his old, shaggy dog over to the motel to be groomed by Karen.

He would always make the appointment for ten o'clock and then come in one or two hours early. He was fully content just to sit in the lobby and watch Karen work for hours at a time, perhaps reflecting on other times, of days long past. Sometimes he would come in without his dog and explain that he was out getting his exercise and stopped by to rest. He would rest while watching Karen.

We also watched and couldn't help but smile as the old man quickly adjusted his bifocals when Karen had to reach for something and the hem on her hot pants rode up, exposing a generous portion of her thigh.

I remember his wife coming with him once and remarking that she couldn't understand why he insisted on having their dog groomed so frequently. I just smiled.

Except for our dog groomers, we prefer to hire inexperienced personnel and train them ourselves. There are too many bad practices in the industry that become ingrained, and many experienced kennel workers fail to share our concerns for the little things we consider important.

As time has passed, I have learned that an employer can have years of experience and all kinds of college degrees, but can still learn from his employees.

One day, an employee came to me and told me that

Mary Ann, one of our attendants, was in the lunchroom crying uncontrollably. I immediately went in and asked if there was anything I could do for her. She shook her head no and continued to cry.

I learned that one of our clients had boarded her elderly dog with us and then had made arrangements with a veterinarian to have it euthanized. Instead of taking the dog to his clinic, the veterinarian did the job in the dog's room at our motel. The dog was in Mary Ann's kennel, and she had insisted on sitting next to it and holding its head on her lap while it was put to sleep.

I was outraged that this veterinarian had carried out his orders on our premises, and without thinking, I directed my anger toward Mary Ann.

"Why in the hell did you stay in the room if it affects you that way?" I demanded.

Without removing the crumpled handkerchief from her eyes, she began to explain. "Mr. Leeds, a few years ago I had an elderly aunt who was very ill. She had actually raised me and loved me more than anyone else in the world. The only thing she looked forward to each day was my visit with her when I got home from school. She had this terrible fear that I wouldn't visit her and that she would die without having anyone near her.

"One weekend I planned to attend a dog show in a nearby town and my aunt begged me not to go. She was so scared that she would die while I was gone. I was young and I wanted so much to go to that dog show. I kept assuring my aunt that nothing was going to happen, and when the weekend came, I went with my girlfriends to the dog show.

"When I returned Sunday evening, I learned that my aunt had died. She died alone, calling my name."

The tears began to well up again in her already reddened eyes. "It wasn't right, Mr. Leeds. Nothing is so important as a living thing. No one should have to die alone, not even a dog."

Before this incident, whenever we were instructed to take someone's pet to a clinic to be euthanized, I always delegated it to one of the attendants. It was something I had difficulty dealing with. It affected me and I couldn't help showing my emotions.

I changed after my talk with Mary Ann. Since that time, regardless of the demands on my time, if the occasion arises, I personally take the pet to its veterinarian. I insist on being with the pet, and, so the animal knows he is not alone or friendless, I hold his paw and stroke his head affectionately. I am no longer ashamed to be seen talking to the animal or of the tears that course down my face.

Over the years, I still haven't learned not to cry. I don't think I ever will.

I believe Mary Ann is the kind of person a good pet-care facility has to have. I don't think a company can ever be more than what its employees make it. You can advertise gimmicks and spend money on public relations efforts, but your product and your success ultimately depend on your employees.

# ROOM SERVICE, PLEASE!

It takes a lot of customers to make even a small business a success. Ours came in every color, shape, size, and species, and while their own stories are of interest, the antics of their owners challenge description.

I have always maintained that anyone who owns a pet acts a little deranged at times. But anyone who stays in the pet-boarding business has to be totally insane. Happily, it's a degree of insanity we readily embrace, freely chosen and salubrious in its effect.

Perhaps our biggest problem in the beginning was the public's failure to perceive the pet motel business as a real business. Some people could not conceive of a pet-boarding establishment having regular hours, being closed on a Sunday, for instance, or even in the evening.

People frequently came at all hours of the day or night to collect their pets. On one occasion, an irate pet owner called the state police, and I had to explain in front of the officers why our offices were closed at 11:00 P.M. on a Sunday. It's a problem every kennel experiences, and it still happens to us every once in a while.

Another time, the president of one of Chicago's largest banks woke up our manager at 1:30 A.M. to retrieve his dog. He and his wife had just flown back from a two-week vacation, and she couldn't bear to be without her dog for a few more hours. It amazes me how people can manage to separate themselves from their pets so they can go off on vacation, yet they can't live another moment without the pet when they return home.

Afterward, I wished I had asked this executive if he would come down and open his bank for me at 1:30 A.M. if I got lonely for my money some morning.

When the kennel is closed and the lights turned down, the animals finally relax, stop their barking, and settle down for the night. The moment you enter the kennel to put a dog in or to take one out, you wake up every dog in the place. It's a trip from perfect silence to total bedlam. Dogs are yelping, jumping up and down, urinating, defecating, tipping over water dishes. By the time you've gotten someone's dog for him, the entire kennel is a total stinking disaster. It's another needless hour of labor for which you are not compensated. Running a kennel is often a twenty-four-hour job, and every moment of freedom is cherished by those who shoulder the responsibility.

Many kennel owners are resolving this problem by posting a notice that there is a twenty-five-dollar charge to pick up a pet when the facility is closed. For some mysterious reason, most pet owners suddenly find they can endure the separation for a few more hours when the alternative involves a charge. Still, there are some who will pay the twenty-five dollars. I tried this procedure only once. The first person to come under the new rule turned out to be a judge who wanted to pick up her dog on a Sunday. She explained to me that she had no alternative but to pay the twenty-five dollars since she lived forty miles away, and she had to be in court all day Monday. I felt so guilty when I heard her story that I gave her the money back and threw away the sign.

Although there are animal attendants on our premises Sundays and holidays, they have other work to do and are not versed in our office procedures. It requires a trained receptionist to do the job properly. Checking a pet in or out is not such a simple task. Medication and dietary requirements must be properly documented. The pet's condition has to be checked for specific details, and vaccinations must be carefully verified. In addition, since the computerized registration system is closed down, there is no cash available for making change. A myriad number of other details must be attended to, and an untrained person cannot do them properly. As dedicated as our office employees are, few volunteer to come in during their off-hours without adequate extra compensation. Even if they agreed to come in, state law requires that they not only be paid, but at the overtime rate as well.

The desire of owners to be reunited with their pets as soon as possible tells us something of the romance between Americans and their pets. Whether it's a reflection on the family of today or not, I don't know, but many couples will rush from the airport to pick up the family pet but will leave the children at Grandma's for one more night.

The relationship between some people and their pets taxes the imagination. My psychic colleague, Beatrice Lydecker, isn't the only one who holds conversations with animals. In my experience, I found that most pet owners talk to their pets, although in a recent study, only 80 percent admitted to it. Certainly, almost all of our customers talk to their pets, and a few hold extended conversations. They even ask their pets' opinions on certain matters, and, what is even stranger, they may take their pets' advice.

We always encourage people to come in and take a tour of our facilities prior to boarding their pets, but we try to discourage them from bringing their pets with them. Sometimes this is impossible. Every once in a while, a dog owner will insist on touring the kennels with his or her dog, and if there is no other way, we permit it.

After the tour, most pet owners will make their reservation. Occasionally, though, the owner will look at the receptionist and say, "No, Fifi says she wouldn't be happy here."

It's a real blow to our ego. We think we have the world's finest pet-care facilities, and this pampered poodle tells its owner that we're not good enough. I always have a nagging suspicion that when he goes home, this poodle runs around his neighborhood bad-mouthing us.

As we were becoming established, we had a disproportionate share of first-time boarders. For years, their owners had brought Grandma in from the Coast to baby-sit the dog or packed Bowser into a crate and took him along. Now, although apprehensive, they came to the pet motel.

Pets are brought in accompanied by an unbelievable quantity of luggage. Three or four pages of typed instructions tell exactly how owners expect their pets to be cared for: special medications, special diets, special treats, special grooming, exercising, teeth brushed after each meal, and so forth. Visitors stand in the lobby and are awed by what they see. There's the German shepherd checking in with a six-pack of beer. He's to get a half a glass every night at bedtime. And the cat with two six-packs of chocolate milk, one can for each day of its stay. The television show, "Real People," was photographing in our lobby that day, and the crew interrupted their filming to include the cat in the program.

And then there was the lady who instructed me to have her dog's behind wiped with toilet paper after each elimination. The first few times it happened, I thought it was strange. Now, I don't even blink. It's a mad, mad, but wonderful world.

One of our frequent guests is a huge St. Bernard whose owner, a doctor, is greatly concerned for her health. Brandy begins each day in our Regency Suite at 8:00 A.M., with a breakfast fit for a queen. She gets three strips of lean bacon, fried crisp, and three scrambled eggs. Don't mix the bacon with the eggs, we were told, or Brandy won't eat them. At 9:00 A.M., Brandy gets a pound of sliced roast beef (medium), and at 10:00 A.M., she gets our regular serving of beef protein dog food.

I doubted that Brandy would decline her breakfast just because the eggs were mixed with the bacon, but I have been assured by our director of animal welfare that a new employee did mix the food on one occasion and Brandy indeed declined to eat it.

Brandy's visits are always rather a hardship for me. I seldom eat breakfast, and when the aroma of bacon and eggs comes wafting through the building, my stomach begs to be appeased. Apparently I am not the only one; on more than one occasion I have caught the attendant munching an extra piece of bacon while preparing Brandy's breakfast.

One time, the doctor brought in a little three-legged

table for Brandy to eat her meals from because she had a sore neck. I don't know how the doctor could tell Brandy had a sore neck, but if he was correct about the bacon and eggs, I wasn't going to question the sore neck.

One of my favorite customers is an elderly lady who visits relatives in Germany every other year. When she brings her dachshund in for boarding, she always brings in an ample supply of beer sausages as well. They are the spicy, garlic-laden salami sticks that many taverns offer their patrons. "At home, Schnapsy always gets a piece of beer salami before going to bed." So, at the pet motel, Schnapsy always gets a piece of beer salami before going to bed!

One dog gets an ice cream soda each night, while another gets a Hostess Ding Dong on Sundays. A dish of ice cream on Sunday is a very common request.

I am not belittling or making fun of these owners or their pets. I firmly believe there is a logic behind it. We develop certain routines with our pets that are mutually rewarding. The pets love the extra attention, and we receive the satisfaction of watching our pets enjoying themselves. I would never even dream of arriving home from the pet motel at night without a Milk Bone for each of my dogs. Like other pet owners, I know they expect it.

One of the things an owner experiences when he boards his pet is the fear that the animal will feel it is being abandoned or loved less. By including the little amenities of special treats, a familiar toy, and some-times a familiar piece of clothing, the owner believes the pet will remember him and not feel deserted. I don't know that it works this way, but I do know that the animals look forward to treat time and seem to enjoy it to the fullest measure.

Many pet owners needlessly suffer deep feelings of guilt over leaving their pets. I have witnessed a number of emotion-packed partings, and I have seen grown men and women break down and cry as they left their pets. One of the most poignant partings I can recall was that of a priest and a young Doberman pinscher that he had adopted from a dog pound only a few weeks before.

After closing the gate to the dog's room, the priest

and the dog stood facing each other on opposite sides of the gate. The priest asked over and over again if the dog might forget him since they had been together such a short time. Each time, the attendant assured the priest he needn't worry. Finally, the priest commented to the attendant, "He really should have something of mine so he won't forget me."

With that, he removed his pair of highly polished shoes, set them at the edge of the dog's bed, and walked to his car in his stocking feet.

That night, when I made the last bed check, I found the puppy sound asleep with his head nestled between the two shoes.

Actually, many pet owners would be mortified if they knew how short a time their pet missed them. It is true a dog or cat may spend one or two days adjusting to its new environment. But by the second or third day, if the boarding facility is any good, the pet will be completely fascinated with all the different smells and sounds. It's the attendant bringing the bowl of food, the terrier in the next room, or the cute poodle across the way that totally absorbs its attention. The pets are sitting by their gate thinking of the three o'clock cookie break, not of their masters who are sitting in a hotel room worrying about them.

However, there are exceptions, and that is why the selection of a good boarding facility is so important.

Our employees know that their first obligation is to the animal's well-being. If they see a dog curled up in a corner of its run, shaking like a leaf, they are expected to go into the dog's room, sit down, and begin socializing with the animal. It's surprising what a comforting hand and a reassuring voice can do.

We have dogs that repeat this behavior every time they come in. Each time we go through the same process of socialization to get the pet adjusted to kennel routine. The results over the years prove it works.

Take Duchess Denton, for example, a timid and nervous little chihuahua. Every time Duchess comes in, she nestles her tiny, quivering, one-and-a-half-pound frame into a corner of her run, totally intimidated by the barking of the other dogs. After one of us spends a little time with her, she is suddenly ready to take on the world. She's the first one to yell for breakfast and the last one to stop barking at a newly arrived guest. I guess she figures that if the others can do it to her, she can do it to them. The first couple of times she boarded with us, we had to hand-feed her boneless chicken to get her to start eating. Now when she visits us, she'll eat anything and everything that's set in front of her.

Another way of acclimating our dogs is by piping soft music into their rooms and play areas twenty-four hours a day. Of course, the volume is reduced at bed-time. About nine o'clock each night, we make the rounds and pass out Mother Hubbard Dog Cookies to all our guests. The size of the dog determines the quantity of cookies it receives.

These cookie breaks are something the dogs really look forward to. At the appointed time, they line up at their gates, almost as if they were soldiers on parade. Some of them will roll over or stand on their hind legs and beg, tricks they probably are made to perform at home. Even the most reluctant guest soon joins the parade and is on its way to a comfortable and trouble-free stay.

Special diets and medications are an important part of our responsibilities. All the details are spelled out on special forms so the attendant knows exactly what has to be done and when. Next to each date is a place where the person giving the medicine or diet must sign. In addition, the director of animal welfare has a number of ways to check if things are being done properly. If we tell a pet owner we will do something, we do it.

There have been only two exceptions over the past thirteen years.

The first occurred when an elderly lady brought in her pregnant miniature schnauzer for boarding. The dog was in its later years and probably shouldn't have been bred. Out of her shopping bag the lady produced a large number of plastic containers in which she had frozen a special meal for each day of the dog's boarding.

"She's an old dog, so she needs a lot of vitamins," she explained. "I fixed all these healthy vegetables, which will be good for her, so don't feed her anything else but this."

The first day we set the concoction of Brussels

sprouts, spinach, and other vegetables down in front of the poor dog, I swear it took on a look of total disbelief. It looked down at the food and then up at us and then just stood there in apparent shock.

By the end of the day, the food remained untouched, and I decided an expectant mother deserved something better than greens for dinner. I went into food prep and made a special meal of canned and dry food that I then set next to her dish of vegetables. In the morning, the dog food was completely gone, but the vegetables remained untouched. It was the same story every day, until finally we stopped trying and just fed the dog a standard lactation diet.

When the elderly owner returned for her pet, she was delighted at the dog's healthful appearance. I never mentioned that it was not due to a vegetable diet.

The other exception took place when a lady boarded a beautiful little Yorkshire terrier. The dog weighed only about a pound, and would have fit inside your coat pocket. After registering, the owner set a loaf of white bread on the counter and ordered that the dog only be fed one slice of bread daily. All attempts to reason with her were futile. The dog was not ill, nor was there any other reason to feed it only bread. Even the lady's veterinarian could not offer a reason for such an irresponsible diet.

When the dog was placed in its room, I went back and made sure that its diet was supplemented with a wholesome dog food.

Raising a dog solely on white bread is condemning a dog to a short lifetime of physical problems caused by malnutrition. Sometimes I wonder if we shouldn't license dog owners instead of dogs.

# McDOLLAR'S, THEY'LL HAVE IT THEIR WAY . . . OR ELSE

Despite the added cost of special care and the high cost of maintenance, we ended our first year with only a modest loss. We made a profit our second year, and the most conservative projections told us that we would never lose money again.

We had actually done better than I had anticipated. We had started with a brand-new, untested concept, without any previous experience and without even one prior customer, and had boarding revenues of almost $300,000 the first year.

Our second year's profit would have been much greater had not the results of our architect's plans begun to take their toll.

The biggest problem was our heating and air-conditioning systems, problems only partially remedied by the addition of twenty more tons of air conditioning and the doubling of our heating capacity.

Major ventilation problems arose as the result of the failure to provide adequate space in the ceiling area for the duct work. Possibly to save money, one row of blocks were deleted from the building height, and apparently the heating contractor could not run the flexible ventilation ducts through the ceilings without damaging them. Years later, we discovered hundreds of tears in the duct work through which our heat and air conditioning had been escaping. Two major ducts were found that had not even been connected to anything and that were releasing all their air into the ceiling space.

Exhaust fans began burning out prematurely, and we found that they were nonstandard units that had been manufactured prior to World War II. No existing replacements were available to fit the openings in our metal roofs, and we had to spend additional thousands to have these archaic fans rebuilt.

Use of the wrong primer resulted in the special epoxy paint peeling off the walls in huge sheets. All the paint had to be removed by sandblasting and then replaced, and we were forced to pay most of the cost.

When we found ourselves without water one morning, we called in a contractor who had to dig down through the concrete floor to find the cause. Instead of a broken pipe, he found no pipe at all, just traces of rust. Apparently, a black iron gas pipe had been used for the underground water line and, not being galvanized, it had just rusted completely away. A whole new system had to be installed.

Our high-pressure sanitizing system was not exempt either. It cost almost $43,000 to install and was supposed to utilize a special high-pressure pipe. Although the installers used the correct high-pressure pipe, they used standard low-pressure fittings for all the elbows, and when we had our first cold spell, these fittings began exploding like grenades, sending pieces of shrapnel in all directions. Water from the broken lines sprayed through the ceiling areas, destroying hundreds of ceiling tiles and short-circuiting some of the electrical wiring.

These deficiencies meant that extra personnel, equipment, and supplies always had to be kept on hand to meet the contingencies we knew would arise. Heating and air-conditioning bills ran 500 percent higher than anticipated and approached $50,000 a year.

Of a more ominous nature was the movement of our building walls during the winter months. After only a few winters, entire walls were shifting several inches, opening huge cracks through which the granular insulation poured out. Steel doorjambs were actually twisted out of shape, and it became impossible to open or close exterior doors. Furnaces had to be kept running continuously to provide the minimum heat needed for the animals.

Exterior concrete structures did not fare even that well. Sidewalks crumbled, concrete slabs sunk over nine inches, and some of the run walls collapsed into piles of rubble. Several years later, the original masonry contractor confided to me that he had obtained a total waiver of liability from the architect because he knew the foundations had not been poured to the proper depths. In some places, he admitted, they had poured only a slab and no foundation at all.

It was disheartening, but there was nothing I could do, and as long as I could pay for the repairs and show Ray Kroc a profit, I didn't complain to him. Every projection I made indicated we would become more and more successful as time went on. Unfortunately, I could not foresee what my partner had in mind.

Toward the end of our second year, the prospect of the pet motel becoming extremely profitable was suddenly shattered. Kroc's attorneys sent me a letter enclosing a series of predated demand notes totaling $150,000 with back interest at 9 percent. In addition, I was advised that I would immediately have to begin paying Kroc an extra $8,000 a month for rent.

If we had filled every room in the pet motel, we still could not have paid the $150,000, let alone the $96,000 in rent. To me it was a cold and deliberate breach of everything the Krocs and I had agreed to. Ray had agreed to provide the building money in exchange for 85 percent of the company's stock. I had urged his lawyers to let me bring in other investors and to borrow the construction money from banks while the interest rate was only 5 percent, but they had insisted on using only Kroc's own money. Now he was demanding an exorbitant rent and interest.

I felt the demands were grossly unfair and refused to sign the notes. His lawyers kept writing and calling me. Over and over again, they assured me that the notes were totally meaningless to our company, but were necessary for Ray's income tax. "It's all being done just to provide him more tax shelter," they kept insisting. I refused to be swayed.

Even if the notes were meaningless, the idea of initiating a rental agreement of $96,000 a year was not. Not to me. I was projecting profits but with real estate taxes on a million-dollar building, plus the exorbitant maintenance and utility costs, there was no way I could see us adding an extra $8,000 expense each month.

As I thought about it, it was difficult for me even to conceive of Kroc initiating these demands. Our relationship had been cordial and open, and in view of his and Joan's past assurances, I very much doubted that he would do anything to jeopardize the success of the company.

I refused to sign the notes and asked for a meeting with Ray. I was convinced these demands were not his doing. If they were not, I would trust him to set the accord straight.

It took a few months, but the meeting finally took place in Ray's office at the McDonald's Oakbrook building. Present were his two attorneys, his accountant, Ray, and myself.

Ray was as cordial and friendly as the first time I met him. Something about him encouraged my respect and a sense of loyalty. Instinctively I felt sure he would support me. I really didn't believe the man was capable of lying.

One of Kroc's lawyers began by suggesting that I tell everyone what was bothering me. I could have recited a litany of complaints, but bringing up the building problems would only have exacerbated feelings. Instead, I merely reminded Ray that when we became partners, he offered to put up the necessary money in exchange for 85 percent of the stock and profits. Not at that time and at no time since then had there ever been any mention of a rental charge or interest on his investment. Our written contract, I said, specifically stated that if he had to loan the company money, the interest rate would be 7 percent. Now he was demanding 9 percent.

I also reminded Ray that I had stated in the very beginning that I would not consider any arrangement that called for 100 percent debt financing. It was obvious to me that the huge interest payments associated with 100 percent borrowed money would be an impossible burden and lead to certain failure. Our arrangement was for equity financing—investment capital, not borrowed capital.

When I finished, Ray looked up at the others in the room.

"Hey, when I buy stock in a company, they don't pay me rent for the buildings or interest on my investment. . . ."

Before he could continue, his lawyers and accountant cut him off. "You don't understand," they told him. "Money has to earn money. Money begets money. Why, you could have put your money into tax-exempt bonds and gotten a better return." On and on they went, and Ray sat in his chair without uttering another word.

During the balance of the meeting, he sat there looking down at his desktop while his lawyers and accountant tried to legitimize this act of fiscal piracy.

Without his support I felt lost. Overwhelmed. This whole matter was apparently not his doing, but he would not speak out to stop it. Finally, as if making a magnanimous gesture, one of the lawyers asked me to suggest a rent figure that would be fair.

"None at all would be fair," I replied.

At length, the figure of $5,000 was suggested. They made it sound as if Ray was making a horrendous financial concession. I made some rapid mental calculations. If our growth continued as I had projected, we would be able to afford the extra $60,000 a year. However, it also meant that we would have little to show as profits and my 15 percent of nothing would be nothing.

I didn't expect anything better from them. I kept looking to Ray, hoping he would speak up and come to my defense. He knew what was happening and I'm sure he knew it was wrong. Instead, he just continued to sit there, staring down at his desk.

When I finally got up to leave, I took one last look at Ray. He refused even to glance up. He reminded me of a marionette waiting for some unseen hand to posture him, unable and unwilling to act on his own.

Within a few days, I received a formal notice that we

would henceforth pay a rental of $5,000 a month. Also included was a new set of predated notes, payable on demand, for $150,000. There was one other item. A new note for another $25,000 "to cover back rent" for the months of August through December, and an additional $6,700 for interest.

Although Kroc's attorneys kept reassuring me that the notes were meaningless and only existed for income tax purposes, they finally spelled it out to me in terms I could understand. Either I sign the notes, or Kroc would not build the other two pet motels or support the present one.

I was never able to reach Kroc by telephone again. He was never in when I called and he never returned my calls. It was as if an invisible shroud had suddenly enveloped him. I had seen my mentor for the last time.

I needed another pet motel desperately. A second pet motel would be built without all the mistakes of the first one, and, based on our present experience, would prove how profitable good pet care could be. I told myself that I had no option. I signed the notes. With the stroke of a pen, American Pet Motels went from a very promising enterprise to one burdened by debt and only marginal profitability.

But this would only be temporary. As our services expanded, our occupancy rate continued to grow and at times we would have over four hundred names on a waiting list for rooms.

# 13

# SPECIAL GUESTS—
# SPECIAL PROBLEMS

My planning never anticipated any significant profit from the boarding of miscellaneous animals. Even though there were millions of these animals being kept as pets, I did not know if there really was a boarding market for them. That we did attract such pets in quantities sufficient to make a profit was an added blessing both for us and for the people who needed a place to board them.

Of the many different types of animals we board, none add more color and beauty to the surroundings than do the birds. From tiny finches to huge crested cockatoos and macaws, we have them all. If they are impressive to look at, the price some of the owners attach to them is overwhelming.

I accepted that the affection shown to dogs and cats by their owners often bordered on the bizarre, but I was soon to learn that such concern and affection was not limited to any particular species. Bird owners are no exception.

Although small, our aviary turned out to be a spectacular sight. One of our summer employees was a very talented artist, and for a modest commission he decorated the aviary walls with a mural of a rain forest complete with a waterfall.

While smaller birds are confined to cages, with a few exceptions, larger birds are permitted to stay on their specially built perches, free of any restraints. It is not unusual to have as many as twenty-five birds boarding at one time, and when they begin chirping and singing it is easy to imagine you are witnessing a real wildlife scenario.

The design and beauty of some of the cages and perches often rival that of the birds they hold. Many bird owners take exceptional pride in designing something more unique and more impressive than any they could buy, regardless of the cost.

Vitamins, special imported seeds, and a variety of special diets and tonics are all part of the bird owners' concerns, and they are never reluctant to leave long lists of meticulous instructions with us.

Certain birds have an uncanny ability to mimic different sounds, especially the human voice. On one occasion, this talent scared the daylights out of us. It was about eleven o'clock at night, and I was working in the conference room with the bookkeeper. The rest of the building was dark and totally silent. All of a sudden, we heard a child's haunting voice calling, "Mommy. Mommy." The voice rose and fell in an eerie manner.

The bookkeeper and I looked at each other. "Good Lord, some kid is locked in here." We jumped up, and turning on the building's lights, ran around opening closet doors and calling for the child to come out. Suddenly we heard the voice again, from the direction of the aviary. We walked to the glass doors and looked in. The child's voice was coming from a mynah bird.

The aviary is a favorite stop for the many group tours that visit the pet motel. I take special delight in showing Girl Scouts and Boy Scouts around the motel. I can always count on a loud response when I warn them not to step on any tails when we walk through the alligator pond.

On one occasion, I wanted to show a group of Brownies how well one of our boarding mynah birds spoke. This particular bird was an incessant talker and had a very large vocabulary. I knew the little girls would get a big kick out of him.

I slid open the glass partition and greeted the bird. There was no response. He just cocked his head to one side and stared back at the group. For ten minutes, while the girls looked on, I went through all kinds of verbal antics to evoke a response. It was useless. He absolutely refused. Embarrassed, I apologized to the scoutmaster and girls and suggested we continue the tour. As I turned to leave, the mynah bird in the next cage, whom I have never heard talk, suddenly shrieked, "That bird doesn't talk, stupid!"

The little girls exploded with laughter, but their chaperones probably don't believe to this day that the whole thing wasn't planned.

Some owners are extremely reluctant to leave their birds with anyone, and that we qualify as a boarding facility is a mark of considerable merit. We even had a case where a man living in Texas contacted his mother in Chicago and asked her to check out our facilities. The man had a rare South American macaw that he had trained to speak three different languages. He was considering bringing the bird to our motel while he was away on a three-month trip to Mexico.

Because he was leaving Chicago on a Sunday, when we were closed, he chose to leave his bird with his mother for one day rather than bring the bird in on the preceding Saturday.

On Monday, the mother telephoned and advised us that she wanted to keep the bird for another week before bringing it in. The following day she called back with tears in her voice. She had placed the bird on the floor to acquaint it with her two little dogs. She said they were getting along fine until the telephone rang and she left the room to answer it. When she returned she found that her dogs had eaten the bird.

Whenever I think of that incident, I recall the story about a man who sent his mother a rare bird worth $50,000. When he called his mother to find out if the bird had arrived, she advised him that it had and that she had made a delicious soup from it. The son was shocked and admonished his mother.

"Why did you cook that bird? He was probably the smartest bird in the world. He could speak fifteen different languages fluently!"

"So?" the mother replied. "If he was so smart, why didn't he say something before it was too late?"

Pickles is a Red Lord Amazon parrot that was raised

in a household where the owner enjoys watching daytime television. Apparently, this fascination with soap operas is shared by the bird. When the owner boarded the parrot the first time, we were told that Pickles would be lost without his game shows, especially "Jeopardy." Although there were several other birds boarding during the same period, Pickles just sat forlornly on his perch. The third day, our groomer brought in her portable television set and installed it in the aviary. The change in Pickles was dramatic. He knew the names of the different soap opera characters and you could hear him join in the dialogue from twenty feet away. But his interest was greatest when "Jeopardy" came on. He bobbed and shrieked with more enthusiasm than any of the show's audience or contestants. The bird was a TV addict.

Dog-training classes became another popular activity that drew a lot of spectator attention. Folding chairs had to be replaced by permanent bleachers to accommodate the crowds who came to witness the transformation of unruly dogs into obedient household pets.

It is always a rewarding experience to watch the undisciplined mayhem that characterizes the first night of class turn into an orderly and obedient collection of owners and dogs by the eighth week. Graduation always includes the compulsory wearing of a four-cornered mortis board by each dog. A red, white, and blue tassel, dangling from one corner, denotes the school colors. It is interesting to see old myths destroyed as dogs of all ages and breeds lose their undesirable traits and are transformed into the kinds of pets society can coexist with.

One of the myths that was put to rest is the adage, "You can't teach an old dog new tricks." At the conclusion of each training class, trophies are awarded for the three best-trained students. In the largest class ever graduated, the first prize was won by a six-year-old cairn terrier who was handled by its sixty-two-year-old owner. As the TV crews ground away, the lady only lamented that she didn't know who trained the hardest, she or the dog.

It was another owner who answered the question of who trained whom in her household when she described a problem she was having with her dog. To teach the dog to "speak for its dinner," she said she would get down on her hands and knees, hold the food out of the dog's reach, and bark until the dog barked. Then she would give the dog its food. Now, a year later, her dog refused to touch its food unless she got down on her hands and knees and barked first.

Stories such as this cause our training director to wince in dismay. Bernie Brown is one of the country's foremost dog trainers, and his success has conditioned him to be less than amused at such stories. When it comes to training a dog, Bernie is a perfectionist and he demands the most from his students. His own dog, Champion and O.T. Champion Meadowpond Dust Commander, accrued more points in competition than any other dog to win the Ken-L-Ration Obedience Dog of the Year award for three consecutive years. Man and dog traveled over 40,000 miles and defeated more than 50,000 dogs in 94 obedience trials in order to attain this record. But if this achievement was noteworthy among those who participated in the show-rings, at least one little boy was able to flaw Bernie's remarkable ability.

At a recent show, Bernie handled a huge German shepherd and put the dog through the trial with seemingly flawless execution. At the conclusion the dog was declared the winner with a total of 199½ points out of a possible 200.

Bernie took the dog to the winner's circle to await the photographer, and while standing there, a little boy walked over.

"Is that the dog that won the big show today?" the boy asked.

"It sure is," Bernie replied proudly.

The boy studied the dog for a while and then exclaimed, "He sure is a big dog."

"He sure is," Bernie replied.

Then the little boy looked up at Bernie and asked, "Tell me mister, if you tell your dog to give you his paw, will he do it?"

Bernie had to pause for a while. "Um . . . uh . . . well, no. He doesn't shake hands." Bernie flushed a little. He had brought this dog through months of intensive training but had never bothered to teach the dog such mundane responses as shaking hands. He stood there, chagrined and sputtering, feeling more than a little foolish in front of his youthful inquisitor.

"Huh!" the boy responded. "My dog can."

A smile of self-satisfaction spread across the little boy's face as he turned and marched off into the crowd, leaving Bernie feeling that the mighty had just been humbled.

I think it's safe to say that any dog would be a better pet if it was obedience trained. Like a well-behaved child, a well-trained pet is always a joy to have around. But it was a friend of mine who proved there were advantages most of us would never think of.

I ran into Patricia Widmark at the Cincinnati airport, following our appearance on a local television program about pet care. Pat is one of the country's foremost authorities on dog training and had been on the program with one of Robert Redford's golden retrievers. When Pat's flight was called for boarding, I watched as she attached a seeing-eye harness to the retriever. After adjusting a pair of dark sunglasses over her eyes, she smiled sheepishly as she prepared to lead the dog onto the plane. "I like to fly with my dog near me and this way they never question it."

I smiled at the thought of attempting this deception with my two-pound Yorkshire terrier.

When we take children on our tours of the pet motel, the stables are always a popular sight. For some reason, children—especially girls—have an inexplicable fascination with horses. This fascination does not always extend to those who work around horses. Ask anyone who works in a stable and he or she will tell you that horses are the dumbest of all animals, and equestrians will cite you dozens of reasons why this is so. But, after having boarded a horse by the name of Image, I require more convincing.

Image was my daughter Gail's horse, and while it was one of many we boarded, it was the only one that stayed with us over a long period of years. And it was only after we arranged proper insurance coverage so that Gail could ride the horse on our grounds that she consented to stable it permanently at the pet motel. It was one of those arrangements parents agree to against their better judgment.

Our problems began when Image started forgetting he was a horse and began thinking he was a dog. Image loved dogs. Every evening, when the dog-training class assembled, Image would trot over and join the class. Except for exchanging sniffs, the dogs didn't bother him, and he didn't bother the dogs. But the instructor was bothered. When the dogs were led to the right, Image would walk to the right. When they turned left, Image would turn left. If they were put in the "stay" position, Image assumed the "stay" position. He absolutely refused to keep away from the dogs. In some respects, he was an outstanding student of novice obedience.

As if interfering with our training classes wasn't enough, Image decided that he would rather spend his time in the kennels than in the stable. On one of our busiest afternoons, I had to interrupt my schedule to respond to a frantic alarm that all of the Imperial Kennel dogs were running around loose in the courtyard. Sure enough, there was Image trotting around with a dozen dogs at his side. It was then that we discovered Image had learned how to open the kennel gate latches.

After that episode, with increasing regularity, I would be called by an animal attendant to remove Image from inside one of the kennels or from one of the courtyards.

The horse was uncanny. He would stand behind a building for hours, peering around the corner, watching each attendant's moves. As soon as someone failed to replace a latch promptly, Image would enter the courtyard and begin letting the dogs out of their runs. He was the best friend they ever had. (Accomplice is perhaps a more appropriate term!) No dog ever attacked Image or even chased him. The dogs seemed to sense from the beginning that Image was their friend.

Each time we inaugurated a new device to thwart him, the horse responded with a new stratagem. He learned how to open the feed containers. By standing on his hind legs, he would reach hay that had supposedly been stored beyond his reach. If he became frustrated, he would dine on our pickup van's windshield wipers or a nice section of the motel's bright red roof. Eventually, we had to equip every kennel gate with a latch and pin lock and the perimeter gates with spring-loaded snap locks to discourage his intrusions further.

When we thought we finally had the horse isolated, Image struck back with a vengeance. His first act was to eat all the screens from our barns windows. Then he started on the plastic window frames. It soon looked as if we were either going to have to admit defeat and let him start staying in a dog kennel or ask Gail to board her horse somewhere else.

It was the owner of a nearby stable who told me Image was a very social animal whose only problem was a lack of companionship. "A goat," he said, "would solve all your problems."

With all the mischief that Image had caused, his boarding certainly had not been a profitable experience. Now I was faced with the prospects of investing in a goat just to make a horse happy.

Marc located a goat for sale and I authorized its purchase with the stipulation that he deliver it in our van and not in my personal car. When he returned, I helped him unload the goat and lead it to the stable. To our surprise, there was another little goat standing next to Image. Unbeknown to us, Gail had gone out that same day and purchased a goat. We now had two free-loading goats to feed, in addition to our equine freebooter.

I must admit, though, that this new arrangement was a match made in heaven. Image ceased his mischievous behavior and he and the two goats became inseparable friends. However, his odd antics did not stop.

Shortly after the goats arrived, I was called outside to witness Image walking around the pasture with one of the goats standing on his back. Everyone denied having had anything to do with it, and as it happened again several times during the next few days, we came to accept this as something the two animals arranged between themselves.

Sure enough, one day we saw Image walk over to the

bleachers in the dog-training area. One of the goats climbed the bleachers until he was level with Image and then simply stepped across onto his back. The two would walk around this way for hours.

Over a period of years, Gail found that her job, evening college courses, and social life were leaving her less and less time to spend with Image, and she began hinting that she might find a new home for him. I did little to dissuade her and, in fact, might have even encouraged her a little. When she finally made the decision, I prevailed upon her to make the acceptance of the two goats a condition of the sale. I had nightmares of two goats chewing their way into the kennels and letting all the dogs out.

Unable to bring herself to sell Image to a stranger, Gail arranged with my old friend, Dr. Corbin, to pasture Image on his farm in southern Illinois. She also talked him into taking the two goats. I hope someday he will forgive me.

# 14

# THE WANTED AND
# THE WANTING

For obvious reasons, our policy of declining to board vicious or unmanageable pets is usually rigidly enforced. Not only have our attendants received serious bite wounds from seemingly nice pets, but if a vicious animal requires special attention, it is impossible for us to come to its assistance without exposing our attendants to serious injury.

Sometimes a pet owner knows his or her dog will bite a stranger but is reluctant to tell us for fear that we won't board it. A classic example was the time I took a little chihuahua from a customer's arms. The lady just looked on as the little dog suddenly clamped its jaws on my index finger. The little monster looked me straight in the eye as it pressed its jaws tighter and tighter.

"Oh," the woman exclaimed. "I forgot to tell you that Pepe doesn't like strangers. . . ."

On more than one occasion I have seen one of our attendants with a little dog hanging by its teeth from her hand, while the owner reluctantly admits that the dog sometimes bites.

In the case of small dogs, our employees are big enough and trained enough to handle any situation that comes up, providing the owners let us know about their pet's dispositions before we get bitten.

With large dogs, it is another story. A hundred-pound shepherd or a pit bull can do a lot of damage, and the size of the attendant is superfluous. These are the types of dogs we sometimes must turn away.

Still, there are times when the circumstances have persuaded us to waive this policy. Occasionally, we have regretted it, but in one particular case I am glad we made the exception. At least for the dog there was a happy ending, if not for us.

One day I received a telephone call from a distraught woman. She was married to a career soldier who had served with a guard dog contingent in Korea, during the war. Upon his retirement, her husband had some- how managed to bring the dog back to Chicago with him. Now her husband lay dying in the veteran's hospi- tal, and she was unable to find anyone who would board the dog until she could get her present situation under control.

Due to the circumstances, I agreed to let her bring the dog into our kennel and I gave her my assurance that we would make special arrangements for the dog's care. Since we have special isolation runs, I felt the additional risk was warranted in this one case.

Duke turned out to be an enormous, black, thick- coated German shepherd. Everything about him warned us to stay clear as the lady placed him in his private room and showed him how to go back and forth to his outside run. When she was ready to leave, she knelt down and hugged the awesome beast to her face.

Although his actions were restrained while his owner was present, once she left the area the huge animal went wild and began attacking its enclosure. Though he stretched the chain link wires to their limit, they con- tinued to hold, and after finally exhausting himself, he quieted down for the evening.

Each day I would walk back to his kennel to check that he was eating and to observe him from a distance. After first charging the gate, he would just stand there motionless, his cold, steely eyes staring directly into mine.

I wondered about the patrols he had gone out on while in Korea, how many times his pads had bled from the ice that forms when snow becomes encrusted on the fur between a dog's toes. Most of all, I wondered what

Duke was thinking about as he stared back from his concrete and wire enclosure.

I wanted to open the gate and pat his head, to try to help him understand that although he was once again in a foreign and alien environment, he was among friends. Although I have been able to make up with hundreds of seemingly hostile dogs, I was never able to with Duke.

With one exception, Duke would never let anyone approach him during the many months he was with us. The one exception was a young attendant named Dave Splett. Like the majority of our employees, Dave worked with animals because he chose to, not because it was the most financially rewarding job he could find.

I learned about Dave's conquest in a most disconcerting way. I entered the door to the food preparation room one day and found myself standing only a few feet from where a huge German shepherd was lying. Dave was kneeling next to the dog brushing its thick coat with a slicker brush. The dog raised its head and turned his eyes in my direction, emitting a low, rumbling growl from his throat. It was Duke.

"Down!" Dave commanded. "Dooown," he repeated. The beast turned his head toward Dave, studied him for a few seconds, and then laid his head flat on the floor. As Dave continued his brushing, Duke rolled onto his back and stared at me from his upside-down position. Slowly, I backed out the door and returned to the lobby. I knew I didn't have to check on Duke anymore. He had accepted a surrogate master.

During the first few months, although the owner checked frequently on Duke's progress, she neglected to send in her payment. Although the reasons were plausible, the routine was becoming painfully familiar. When some months later the visits ceased completely, an enquiry revealed that her husband had passed away and the woman had just picked up in her mobile home and left town.

Duke was not the first dog abandoned at the motel, nor would he be the last. Legally, we follow a procedure of sending a registered letter to the owner's last known address, and if we do not receive a reply within ten days, we are free to dispose of the pet. In Duke's case, finding a home for him was out of the question. The only alternative was putting him to sleep. It was an option I could not bring myself to take.

While our business was good, our financial obligation to the Krocs was still a major consideration. When Duke's boarding bill reached $1,000, I pulled his folio and stopped adding in the daily charges.

Several enquiries failed to furnish any information on the owner's whereabouts. I knew we could not afford to continue keeping a nonpaying guest, but neither could I turn this one out. Each week I would postpone the final action for another week, and then another. I began again to make my daily pilgrimages to visit Duke. He was not as hostile as he once was and I would sit down on the concrete floor just outside his gate and talked to him for long periods of time.

"It wouldn't be right," I kept telling myself. Here was a dog that had served our country while I was home enjoying the benefits. He required so little, after having given so much. It didn't seem right that he should be condemned to death because he couldn't pay for a warm room and a few handfuls of dog food. After each visit, I would walk back to my office and postpone again the decision I knew had to come.

Over a year later, I was summoned to the telephone by a call from a priest at the nearby Glenview Naval Air Station. He told me he had received a letter from Duke's owner asking him to please find out if Duke was still alive, and if so, if there was any possibility she could get her dog back. She had finally settled down in a mobile home park in Florida, but had no money with which to pay Duke's boarding bill.

At this time, the bill was over $2,000.

"Father," I replied, "if you can find the means of shipping Duke to Florida, I'll forget the boarding bill."

A week later, Dave took Duke from his run for the last time. We loaded him into one of our largest shipping crates and bade him farewell. Three sailors from the Glenview Naval Air Station loaded the crate into a government station wagon. At the base, Duke was loaded into a waiting Navy transport plane being flown by naval reservists on a training mission, its destination, Florida.

Whether the commandant of the base of any other authorized personnel participated in this action, I will probably never know. From what I was able to learn, it was the effort of a few fine people who wanted to help one of our four-legged warriors go home.

I received one more call from the priest to let me know that Duke had arrived safely and was basking in the Florida sunshine with his owner. He also wanted me to know that the lady had said that if she could ever afford it, she would send us the money she owed.

I smiled at the hopelessness of ever collecting this debt. "Tell her the exact amount is two thousand, one hundred, and twenty-eight dollars and not to worry about it. I won't need the money until 1986." (At the time, I had parted from Ray Kroc and had a balloon payment of $750,000 coming due in 1986.)

Many times it is my own employees who resolve the dilemma of an abandoned pet. Neither their friends nor families are excluded from among the possible sources of a new home. "Just one more pet" is a familiar plea. Peggy and I are not exceptions. In our own home are two West Highland terriers and one two-pound Yorkshire terrier who were abandoned by their original owners. Another abandoned dog, a huge malamute, strolls the grounds of the pet motel, a permanent mascot without portfolio.

There are a number of reasons people give up their pets, but, to me, abandonment is the cruelest answer of all. Over the years we have heard many excuses, but few justify the act. For many abandonments do not end happily.

Occasionally, someone will bring a dog to the pet motel in the middle of the night and leave it tied to our entrance gate. Sometimes there is a note asking us to take good care of it, but more often, there is just a poor, cowering, bewildered animal.

I recall driving in one bitter, cold morning to find an old Great Dane tied to our driveway gate. The gray hair around his eyes and muzzle confirmed his advanced age. He was terribly thin, and the callused folds of skin on his elbows indicated the dog had been sleeping on concrete for a long time.

I untied the dog and led him into the nearest empty extra-large Imperial room. It was a Tuesday, and I knew the room probably wouldn't be needed until Friday. For a few days at least, the old dog would know the comfort of carpeting and a foam-rubber mattress.

I made out a diet card calling for ample mixed canned meat and our regular dry dog food. The old dog ate like it was his first meal in weeks. We fed him three meals a day, and the dog walkers took him out for long walks on our back acreage. He didn't move any faster when the animal warden called for him on Friday, but he did appear several pounds heavier and a little more contented.

Ironically, the following morning I received a telephone call from a man who was enquiring about the dog. He claimed he had given his dog to some boys who had agreed to give it a home. He didn't explain how he knew the dog was at the pet motel, nor did I ask him. All I did was tell him that the dog had been turned over to the dog pound, and if he hurried, he might be able to retrieve it before it was euthanized.

There are other pet owners who check their pets into the pet motel and then never pick them up. For some reason, these are almost always dog owners, very rarely cat owners. Over the years, we have learned to recognize the profile this type of person fits. Invariably, he or she is either moving or in the process of getting divorced. Women seem to abandon more pets than men, perhaps because of poorer economic situations. Sometimes it's because of a landlord's restrictions, and often because a parent has ordered the son or daughter to get the pet out of the house.

When a problem is apparent, we ask for a sizeable deposit. However, this does not always discourage people. Some are natural con artists who aren't the least inhibited from going the limit. They will not only give you the information you seek, they will offer their minister as a reference. Of course, the information is all erroneous. They'll put their dog in the most expensive suite, order special diets, exercising, and grooming, all with no intention of paying. Perhaps they feel that as

American Pet Motels, Prairie View, Illinois

Socrates shows affection by using my arm as a teething ring

Socrates is caught trying to figure out the combination to the refrigerator

Partners in the grand opening of a grand adventure in pet care (from left, Robert Leeds, Joan Kroc, Ray Kroc, Peggy Leeds)

Checking in

A guest stands guard over his luggage

Beauty treatments are given in the motel grooming salon

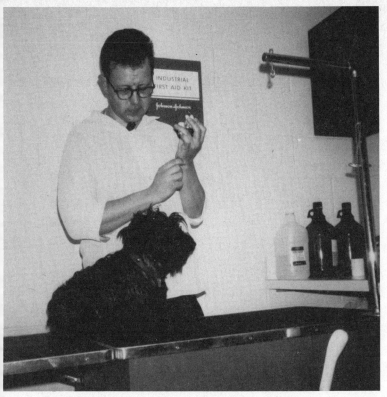

One of the veterinarians prepares to update a guest's vaccinations
in the service clinic

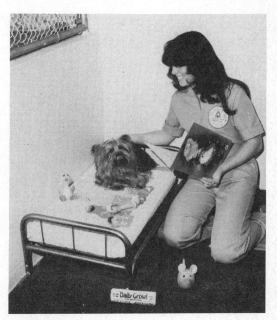

A pampered guest is read a
greeting card from his owner

After a stay at the motel, a guest is delivered home in the pet limousine

Nicki, a ten year old malamute
was abandoned at the pet motel
six years ago and is now
the motel mascot

Image, the horse that thought he was a dog, with Gail Leeds

A cat has a visitor in one of the Imperial Suites

Peggy and I receive a twenty-five pound Christmas present from the staff

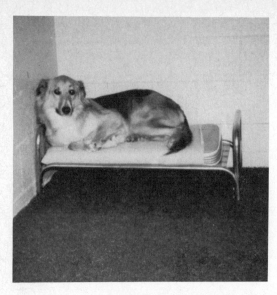

A guest enjoys his "Poochie" foam
mattress and brass bed

Even a rat needs love and affection

Turtles are frequent guests

Karen, the motel's groomer, bathes
one of the guests

A baby hyacinthine macaw observes the aviary from the top of its cage

Charly, an Amazon parrot, enjoys a ride on an attendant's shoulder

The owner finds her bird reluctant to leave the motel Aviary

Reinecki, an Arctic fox, during one of his many visits to the motel

A primate guest checks out a hastily prepared hammock for a stay at the motel

Tiger and Tiddles have their nap interrupted for luncheon

Enjoying the view from the top perch of her apartment

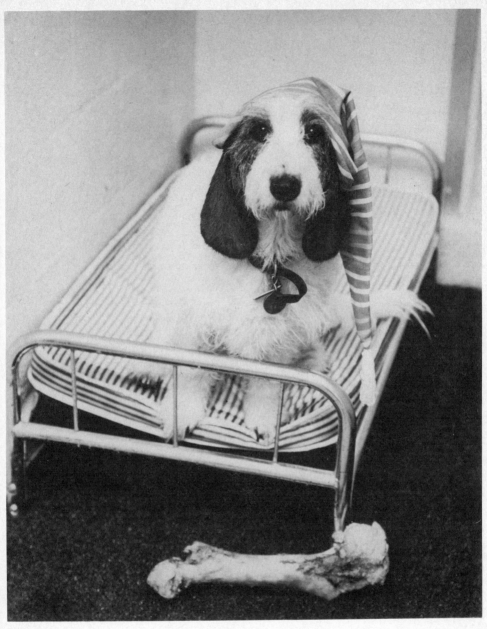

Bedtime

**Ready to be tucked in for the night**

long as they are abandoning the pet, they shouldn't scrimp on their parting gesture.

What they fail to consider, or perhaps don't care about, is that everyone else—the groomer, the dog walker, all of us—loses. And, in the end, the pet loses, too. Recently, many communities have begun passing ordinances to deal with people who abandon their pets. We now have the promise that our own local authorities will vigorously prosecute any individual who abandons an animal. It is a good ordinance and long past due.

But not all abandonments are so cruel.

Over the past several years, there has been an increasing tendency for older people to move from private dwellings to apartments and condominiums, some of which have restrictions against the keeping of pets.

At least once a month we receive a call relative to perpetual boarding, and while to many the cost may seem high, we now have several permanent guests who will live out the balance of their lives with us.

While we try to make life for these animals as pleasant as possible, I am sure the transition from a home environment to a kennel has an effect on them. Regardless of all our efforts, no substitute exists for the emotional warmth of a family environment. In the home, a pet will seek out its master when it desires attention or just the simplest affection. In a kennel, this is not always possible.

To ease the transition, we encourage our employees to spend extra time with these pets. They are taken from their rooms and played with, fed extra and given treats, and are regularly groomed or bathed at our expense. On occasion, one of us will take a pet home for a few days to let it share again the family experience. With all the extra services, we sometimes question whether we're making any money on these pets. I've never checked. To the consternation of my partner, I really don't want to know, nor do I care.

Two of our permanent boarders were not really abandoned. They were picked up from a veterinary hospital in accord with some telephone instructions from a lady who said she was elderly and could not care for them in her own home.

Since that time, I have learned that she has at least a

dozen dogs boarded around the Chicago area. All of the dogs are strays that she found, and rather than turn them over to the dog pound and possible death, she has them checked by a veterinarian, treated if necessary, and then boarded in a kennel to live out their natural lives.

Although I have corresponded with her, I still have never met or spoken with her since our initial contact. I have no conception of her financial means, but assume that the bills for keeping all these strays must be considerable. Each month her check arrives on time, and occasionally she includes a short scribbled note about Daisy, Snoopy, or one of her other four-legged orphans. I often think about this lady and hope that her fellow human beings provide as well for her as she provides for these strays.

Sometimes something will happen that gives me reason to wonder how some people can behave as they do. Among our more affluent customers was a couple who boarded their miniature schnauzer quite often because of their frequent trips. One day I commented on the fact that the dog had been with us for an unusually long period of time. I was then advised that Sparky was being boarded on a permanent basis.

Apparently her owners had won over a million dollars in a sweepstakes and had moved to Arizona to retire. Because the condominium they purchased didn't permit pets, they had elected to abandon the dog that had been their faithful companion for so many years.

Sparky boarded well for the first several months, but then we noticed a gradual deterioration in her appearance. Her appetite kept decreasing, and on some days she refused to eat at all. Her movements became more labored, and she began acting more and more as if she had lost interest in living. Nothing we did seemed to stem the process.

I began having Sparky brought up to my office, where she would spend the day with me. She was extremely well behaved and, surprisingly for a schnauzer, rarely barked. Except to go to her water bowl or food dish, she seemed almost content just to lie at my feet until the time came to return to her room.

At home, I began talking about Sparky with increasing regularity, until at last I prevailed upon Peggy's sentimental nature to such an extent that she suggested I bring Sparky home for the weekends. My own dogs, Casanova and Koira, were both quite accustomed to my bringing stray dogs into the house, so they offered no resistance to the newcomer.

At first, Sparky was a little frightened and shy, but over the next few months her appetite and spunky behavior began returning. She soon learned how to jump up on the furniture, and we started awaking with three dogs in our bed instead of two. Gradually, too, her coat returned to its former lustrous condition, and her behavior matched that of our own two dogs. In fact, when I opened the patio door, there was general mayhem as the three dogs vied with each other to be the first through the opening.

One day, her owners returned to Chicago and called for Sparky. They took her to a veterinarian and had her put to sleep. They explained that boarding her was too expensive.

I will never be able to understand people like this. I am sure that, had the circumstances been reversed, the most wretched cur would have turned down any amount of money before it would have given up its friends.

There are other occasions when the decision to arrange for lifetime boarding has been an act of compassion. Sometimes sick or elderly persons will want to make a provision for the continued well-being of their pet, in contemplation of their own death. Regrettably, where there are heirs, greed and avarice are frequently sufficient motivation for having this provision set aside. Then it is only a matter of time before we receive a court order directing us to have the animals put to sleep. In only one case did the attorneys permit us additional time in which to find the dog a home.

The result of one such case was so tragic that it will haunt me the rest of my life.

Late one April, I received a telephone call from an elderly lady who was entering a hospital for major surgery. Arrangements were made for us to pick up her two German shorthair pointers and board them until she recovered. The dogs had been her husband's most cherished possessions, and since his death had become this lady's constant solace.

When she talked with me, her concern was not about herself or the pending surgery, it was only for the two dogs. Aware that her situation was tenuous, she explained that in the event anything happened to her, she had appointed her sole nephew as the administrator of her estate and that adequate arrangements had been made for the continued welfare of the two dogs at the pet motel.

She left no doubt in my mind that, more than anything else in the world, her preoccupation was with the welfare of her husband's dogs.

Apparently, the operation was successful, but the general health of the lady declined to the point where she was unable to return home. Eventually she was transferred to a nursing home, and although her condition continued to deteriorate, she never failed to telephone each week to enquire about the welfare of Victoria and Hannibal.

During the last few months, her telephone calls became less frequent and her voice more distant and rambling. She would keep me on the telephone for long periods of time, recounting memories of her husband and the two dogs and the happy times they shared.

Regardless of how busy I was, I accepted, as a personal obligation, the duty to take her calls. As we grew more familiar, I began chiding her for her needless concerns and sternly lectured her to follow her doctor's advice so she could hurry home to Hannibal and Victoria.

Then, one day I received a telephone call from the law firm that represented the lady's nephew. The nephew had had his aunt declared incompetent, and in exercising his power as administrator, had obtained a court order to have the two dogs destroyed.

It was not a question of there not being enough money for both the nephew and the dogs' maintenance; it was a question of greed.

There was no alternative to the court's order. Both dogs were surrendered to a veterinarian and I held each one as the lethal dose of liquid was injected.

It was not the end of the incident. Although the lady was supposedly incompetent, from time to time she still telephoned me to enquire about the dogs and just to talk.

I hadn't the heart to tell her of her nephew's perfidy, so instead, I lied to her. I told her that I had placed the two dogs with a friend of mine who had a large farm in Wisconsin. I told her how the dogs loved to romp through the wide, open fields and how much better they seemed since regaining this measure of freedom. It seemed like such an insignificant sin and one not altogether unworthy. Finally, after a few more weeks, the telephone calls ceased completely. I thought the nightmare was finally ended.

I was wrong.

Almost three months had gone by when I suddenly got a call from a voice that was vaguely familiar. My heart almost stopped when the caller vigorously identified herself as the owner of Hannibal and Victoria.

"Mr. Leeds," the voice said joyously. "I beat him. I beat my nephew!"

She then told me that she had made up her mind to get better and she had done so, to the extent that she was able to have the court declare her sane and competent. She was now coming home and she asked me to deliver her two dogs the following day.

I was stunned by the turn of events. No one had told her that the two dogs had been put to sleep. I didn't know what she remembered about what I had told her, but I could not continue the charade. The only thing I could do was tell her the truth. It was one of the hardest things I have ever had to do.

There was silence at the other end of the line. Then her voice choked up, and I heard her crying uncontrollably.

"He tried to steal everything from me. Do you know what my nephew did, Mr. Leeds? He bought himself automobiles with my money, and he went on trips to Europe. But you shouldn't have let him do that. You shouldn't have let him kill my dogs, Mr. Leeds. You shouldn't have let him kill them. Why did you lie to me? Why did you let him do it?"

Her voice trailed off and I heard the line disconnect.

117

She called again later in the day and then the next day and the next week. For months after she would call me. Like a voice coming out of a fog, she would interrupt her crying to ask me, "Why did you let him do it? Why did you let him kill Hannibal and Victoria, Mr. Leeds. Why?"

She hasn't called for several years now, but within my own mind the telephone continues to ring and I hear her distant voice crying and asking me, "Why? Why, Mr. Leeds? How could you let him do it?"

# 15

# VIRUS STRIKES
# THE CATTERY

Within two years, we were boarding ten thousand dogs and cats a year plus hundreds of exotic pets, and though we encountered problems, the catastrophe the experts predicted never materialized.

As time went on, experience confirmed that the number-one hazard of boarding was stress. Illness, injury, and death were more the product of inadequate care, rather than normal circumstance.

One such hazard that we refuted was what the trade referred to as "the collie syndrome."

"You cannot board collies," I was warned. "They won't eat and they'll just pine away and die on you."

It was pure nonsense. Over the years, we boarded every kind of dog and cat, including thousands of shelties and collies, and we never had one pine away and die. The idea that you can't keep dogs from dying of "grievance disease" is absurd. Actually, there is no such thing as grievance disease, except in the minds of those too incompetent to recognize and treat the problem of stress.

Stress may account for as much as 90 percent of boarding problems, but it can be dealt with by kennel operators who will take the time and effort to minimize it.

There are many kennel operators and veterinarians who never visit their facilities on Sundays and holidays. Animals, sick and healthy ones, are cooped up in cages, where they are forced to eat, sleep, and eliminate, without any human attention, sometimes for more than two days. They are neither fed nor given their required medication. Their cages are not cleaned, and they are forced to wallow in their own waste until the next regular work day.

This is the real reason many boarding facilities will not permit you to see where your pet is housed, and it is often the real reason they require that your pet be bathed before you can pick it up. They do not dare let you see the animal, so encrusted with urine and feces, until it is cleaned up.

I have heard the specious argument that it is good for an animal to go without eating one or two days a week. I have heard people recommend this same practice to other people. "It is good for you to purge your intestines by fasting one day a week."

I have yet to see one piece of scientific data to support this claim. In the wild, an animal will gorge itself, and then may not eat again for several days, but usually because it's either not hungry or because food is not readily available. No one has ever shown me a dog or cat that regularly declines to eat every seventh day of its own choice. It is the opinion of many that such a practice is the result of penny pinching, rather than concern for the pets' welfare.

There is another widespread misconception rampant in the boarding industry that accounts for the illness and death of many pets. This is the mistaken belief that if a pet doesn't eat at first, it will eventually get hungry enough to eat anything you offer it. Too often this can lead to tragic consequences. Because of stress, an animal can, and often will, continue to refuse food until it begins dehydrating, sometimes causing irreversible organ damage. It literally will starve itself to death even though food is available.

One of our most valuable tools is a "report card" kept for each of our guests. The attendant records how much food the animal eats each day on this card, as well as the condition of its urine and stool. Space is also provided to note any changes in the pet's "personality," which is often an indication that it is not feeling well. Experience has taught us the importance of a pet eating regularly if it is to stay healthy.

To assure that this happens, we adopted a strict policy regarding our pets' eating regimen. Young dogs and cats must eat a full meal by the third day of boarding, and pets eight years of age or older must eat a full meal by their second day.

The task of enforcing such a policy is a little more arduous than it sounds. Being suddenly plucked from the security of its own familiar surroundings and placed in a strange confinement, amidst strange people and animals, some pets will refuse to eat even the same food they receive in their own homes. This situation calls for a variety of ploys and subterfuges.

Most problem dogs can be successfully motivated by starting them out on a can of cat food. I suspect the strong fishy aroma has something to do with the reason so many of them will accept this alternative. If that fails, Mighty Dog, a dog food manufactured by the Carnation Company, and that must be a very close approximation of human food, usually succeeds. Our next recourse is cooked hamburger or leftovers from our own dinner table. There are few canines who can refuse Peggy's quiche or one of her other culinary achievements.

For those rare pets who decline the Leeds' gastronomical enticements, substantial doses of vitamin-laced Nutri-Cal are given, and as a last resort, an injection of Vitamin $B_1$ by a veterinarian has never failed to achieve the desired results.

I have often heard pet owners complain that they boarded their pet with someone and the dog or cat had been deliberately starved. I doubt that this was the case. Loss of weight while being boarded is frequently not an indication that the animal didn't eat well. On the contrary, it may have eaten twice as much as it did at home.

In fairness to kennel operators everywhere, pet owners should be aware that there are some dogs who will eat like pigs while in a kennel and still lose weight. Some breeds, particularly German shepherds, Irish setters, and Great Danes may become so stressed that their metabolism speeds up and their systems start pumping out adrenaline, causing them to burn up all their caloric intake.

The worst case we ever had was a huge German shepherd that was boarded with us for several months while its owners were in Europe. He was a very nervous dog and would rarely lie down or relax. He was fed our normal diet, but after only a week, we noticed a significant weight loss. A fecal exam confirmed that the dog did not have any intestinal parasites, so we had nothing to blame the weight loss on other than stress.

We increased the quantity of food and added an afternoon and evening feeding. It was three times what we normally fed a dog that size, but even so, he continued to lose weight.

We were feeding the dog two pounds of canned dog food, two pounds of high-protein dry dog food, and two pounds of cottage cheese a day and he ate every bit of it without getting sick. Still, we could not put any weight back on him. We tried every old remedy anyone suggested. Honey, molasses, garlic, and dozens of health-food supplements all failed.

Finally, we called the veterinary college at the University of Illinois.

"Give up," they counseled. It was impossible for the dog's system even to process all the food we were feeding it. Most of the food was going right through him without benefiting him at all.

In the end, we cut his ration down to three pounds of food a day, but over the next several months, despite continued efforts, we were unable to restore the dog to its former weight.

When the owners called for their dog, they were outraged. Despite our explanation of all the efforts we had made, they threatened to sue us for having mistreated their dog. A week later, one of them telephoned to advise me that the dog had completely regained the lost weight and the matter was forgotten. I have seen this problem numerous times. Some pets will always lose weight in a kennel, but when they return to their home environment, they will regain it in a surprisingly short time. I can only attribute it to the stress the animal is in when it is away from its family.

Problems like this would rarely occur if people socialized their pets more during their formative years. Exposure to other people and lots of human attention helps develop a good personality in a pet. There are many in this industry who believe a neurotic pet is often a reflection of the environment it is brought up in. Pets that are boarded while they are young actually learn to enjoy the experience and fare very well when left alone by their owners.

With the report card, we were able to catch minor problems early and as they were treated immediately, more serious problems virtually disappeared.

Unfortunately, the cost of having veterinarians treat even minor problems added another financial burden, and there were some who argued that since these problems were not within our control, the costs should be passed on to the pet owners. I disagreed. Even though it was fair, I knew it would upset some customers to come home and find a veterinary bill in addition to their boarding bill.

Except where there was a veterinary record of previous treatment available to us, it was virtually impossible to determine if some conditions existed prior to boarding. Arguing each case risked offending our clients and damaging our reputation. I didn't want to do what some of the other kennels were doing. I wanted to do better!

Our Pet-I-Care warranty was revised to include reimbursement for any illness, injury, or death, regardless of cause. Although certain limits and exceptions were kept, a preexisting illness was the only exclusion. Even fleas and ticks were covered, and because a condition sometimes showed up after a pet had left the motel, we even extended the coverage to include a reasonable period of time after the pet had gone home.

We knew that offering to pay for any kind of a problem could become a Pandora's box. Ninety-nine percent of the complaints were about problems over which we had no control. A dog would injure its feet by trying to dig through the concrete floor in its room, or damage his tail by swinging it back and forth against a wall. And sometimes a dog would get diarrhea or begin vomiting because its owner fed it or gave it too much water immediately upon bringing it home from boarding. But regardless of the cause of a problem, we wanted to give pet owners financial protection for the first time.

For the most part, the warranty has worked far better than anticipated. The nice thing about it is that the pet owner does not have to prove any liability. If any kind of a problem develops, we pay for the veterinary care.

Of course, there are always some people who will abuse an offer like ours. On more than one occasion, a sick pet was deliberately boarded with us in order to get us to pay for the required treatment. It has happened also that an owner will pick his pet up and immediately inspect the animal's body and then point out a hidden sore or wound in some obscure place. If his veterinarian states that he has never treated the animal for this problem, we end up paying for the medical care.

In a few cases, the problem was leukemia, infectious peritonitis, or some other long-term illness that even the owner's own veterinarian confirmed would have been impossible for the animal to contract during the boarding period. In one case, an entire family began making a scene in our lobby, claiming their poor dog had come out of our kennel with a huge tick in its nose. After closer inspection, I advised the family that the problem they were so outraged about was nothing more than a mole that had probably been on the dog's nose for years. None of them had ever noticed it because it was hidden by a tuft of hair.

Problems have been the exception. The vast majority of pets have gone home in as good or better condition than when they came in to be boarded, and most have come back many times. It was one of our receptionists who gave us the idea of celebrating a guest's one hundredth visit by boarding it in a Regency suite and giving it all the amenities available free of charge. It is now a common occurrence. When a Chicago resident recently set a record with United Airlines by flying to all fifty states within a thirty-day period, the public was unaware that during each trip this lawyer's dog was boarded at our pet motel. Over the past ten years, Louki, his large white samoyed, has boarded with us on over two hundred different occasions without suffering so much as a broken toenail. It can be done.

Unfortunately, despite all of our strict requirements and carefully planned procedures, we were not totally immune to the ravages of those common animal diseases that can strike regardless of the precautions taken. One of these, rhinotracheitis, struck us during our second year of operation.

The disease broke out in one cattery and soon spread to all sixty cats in our two catteries. The disease is caused by a virus that affects the nasal membranes of cats and also causes ulcerations of the tongue and mouth. A cat first begins sneezing, then a discharge begins from its nose and eyes, and finally its mouth fills with small ulcerated sores. Once a cat's nasal passages become obstructed, it can no longer smell and will refuse to eat or drink.

With many illnesses, if you can keep an animal eating, it can usually recover. It may take time, but the animal's own body will generate the antibodies necessary to overcome the disease. But, with rhinotracheitis, cats refuse to take nourishment, and the chance of dehydration and subsequent death is a very real threat.

When the disease first broke out, each cat was taken to its own veterinarian for treatment, even though there were six veterinary clinics within a few miles of us. In some cases that meant traveling over sixty miles. Rhinotracheitis was diagnosed and the antibiotic Tylocine and Sulfa, 200mg, and URD, an upper respiratory decongestant, were prescribed. In addition, the need to get food into the cats to sustain them was stressed.

Recognizing that we were going to have a problem getting them to eat on their own, several veterinarians recommended forced feeding. This meant putting a tube down the cat's throat into its stomach and forcing a solution of baby food into the stomach by use of a large syringe.

If the experience was distasteful to us, it was no less unpleasant for most of the animals. We first had to wrap the cat in a towel so it couldn't rip us apart with its claws, and then one person would hold it while another person inserted the tube and injected the food. Some of the cats accepted the procedure stoically, but the majority fought it with a vengeance.

On a couple of our first attempts, a relaxed grip on the cat's muzzle resulted in the mouth closing and the subsequent severing of the rubber tube. Let me assure you, it's a terrifying experience to find yourself staring at the end of an apparatus that suddenly is missing a foot or more of rubber hose of which only a small portion is still sticking out of the cat's mouth.

Fortunately on both occasions that this happened, the missing tubing was retrieved without any untoward effects, and a call to one of the nearby veterinary clinics produced a novel solution, a wooden yoke that fit in between a cat's jaws. A small hole in the center of the yoke permitted the stomach tube to be inserted, and the problem of severed tubes was eliminated.

Despite our best efforts, the disease spread until every cat being boarded was sick. With sixty sick cats, it became logistically impossible to continue to take each one to its own veterinarian for treatment. Instead, we called upon one of the local veterinarians and let him direct the treatment process. There was really nothing he could do other than to furnish us with medicine and advise us to continue with the treatment we were administering.

It was an exasperating period. Each day, we would begin the treatment early in the morning and not finish until late that night. Within a few days, however, we began to see some improvement. Some of the cats began eating on their own, and the visible symptoms slowly began disappearing.

When the owners returned from their vacations and were advised about their cats, only a few were upset, but as might be expected, all were anxious to take their pets home with them right away. Rather than incur the risk of inadequate home treatment, we tried to persuade them to leave their cats with us until they were completely well. We were well aware of how difficult it was to give a cat its pills and also how important it was to monitor how much the cat was eating and drinking. Most owners agreed, but some insisted on taking their cats to their own veterinarians for treatment. In a few cases this was a terrible mistake, but we were powerless to prevent it.

The boarding of cats in cages is such a lucrative practice that many Chicago veterinarians do it for extra income. Because rhinotracheitis is such a virulent disease, some of them refused to hospitalize our clients' cats for fear of spreading the disease to their boarders. Instead, they gave out bottles of pills and sent the cats home. For some, it was a useless gesture. Pilling a sick cat is a skill, and some of the owners could not master it. The end result was the needless deaths of several of the cats.

But of the cats that remained with us, every single one recovered.

We concluded the virus must have been introduced into the motel by one of our feline guests. There was no way we could have prevented the epidemic. Regardless, we paid everyone's veterinary bills plus an additional $250 to owners whose cats died. This was in accord with our Pet-I-Care warranty. What hurt me the most was the evidence that if those cats had been left with us for care, they all probably would have survived.

It was a traumatic experience, both emotionally and financially. No cat-boarding facility in the country had as many safeguards as we did, and still we were vulnerable. It was hard for me to rebut a suggestion that we discontinue boarding felines. All-pet boarding was a concept that I refused to give up on.

The solution occurred within weeks of the incident when Pitman Moore Laboratories announced a new vaccine effective against rhinotracheitis. For the boarding industry, the introduction of this vaccine was a milestone in feline health care. For us it offered salvation. Henceforth, along with rabies and distemper vaccines, all boarding cats would be required to have the rhinotracheitis vaccination.

As an additional safeguard, we required that all vaccinations must be given at least ten days prior to boarding because pets vaccinated with live-virus vaccines may actually shed the virus and infect other animals of the same species. We did not want to take any unnecessary chances. Because this policy is strictly enforced, we occasionally lose the business of a pet owner who prefers to board his pet elsewhere rather than bother with vaccinations. Surprisingly, among the local boarding facilities that do not require vaccinations for rabies, distemper, or rhinotreachitis are several operated by veterinarians.

# 16

# DOGGED BY VETERINARY VENGEANCE

With all the faults and deceptive practices prevalent among boarding kennels, I reasoned that the veterinary community would welcome us and support the concept of good, professional pet boarding.

This was a naive assumption. The shocking conditions I had found in some veterinary boarding facilities (in many cases even worse than those of kennels, since healthy animals were being boarded among sick animals with contagious diseases) should have forewarned me that there would be some veterinarians who would not welcome our kind of competition.

Time would prove that this group would never support us or our objectives. Indeed, they would devote a disproportionate share of their time and ability to opposing any effort to improve the quality of pet care in their area, using the various veterinary associations to do so.

Fortunately, there were other veterinarians who welcomed our arrival. Some were skeptical at first because we promised so much, but after a short time, we began receiving numerous referrals from these veterinarians and developed an excellent relationship with them and their clients.

The majority of veterinarians, though, parochial in

their interests, hardly noticed the arrival in their midst of a revolutionary concept for boarding pets.

From the very beginning, however, the uniqueness of our concept became a media fascination. Not only in America, but in Europe and Asia, our pet-care program was written about in the leading newspapers and magazines and talked about on radio and television.

With our national exposure, the face of the boarding industry began to change. It was more than just a face-lift; it was a major overhaul. Many kennel operators finally began to realize that the boarding of an animal extended beyond just storing the pet until its owner returned. They began dressing up their facilities, installing music, heat, and air conditioning. They started keeping health records and began accepting responsibility for the pets they boarded. It seemed as if half the kennels in America became pet motels overnight. Unfortunately, in many cases, nothing changed except the name.

In April 1979, I received a telephone call from Dr. Robert Mahr, a veterinarian who operated several clinics and kennels northwest of Chicago. Although we were competitors in the boarding business, when questions or problems arose, neither of us was reluctant to contact the other for assistance.

On this occasion, Dr. Mahr offered some information that sent a cold chill through me.

A new and mysterious virus had broken out among dogs in Illinois. A dog that was in apparent excellent health one minute could be dead in a matter of hours. No one knew the cause or how to prevent or cure it. To make matters worse, no one was even sure how the virus was being spread, though veterinarians suspected it was spread in canine fecal matter.

In addition, the disease was extremely contagious, and once it broke out in a community, it spread rapidly among the dog population. Not only had several local kennels already closed down due to the outbreak, but even one of the veterinary hospitals had to close because dogs coming into the hospital for routine vaccinations were becoming infected.

The cost of an outbreak at the pet motel immediately ran through my mind. We were boarding over 260 dogs every day and because of our Pet-I-Care warranty, we could be facing veterinary charges and death benefits of more than $75,000. An outbreak would surely bankrupt us.

I could also imagine the newspaper stories and the public's reaction if we had an outbreak. All of the time, effort, and money we had invested to prove the merits of our concept would fade forever in the face of such a calamity. I knew that we could not afford to sit around and wait.

I began contacting other veterinarians and research laboratories to gather as much information about the virus as possible, hoping someone would know of a preventive measure. Unfortunately, most of the veterinarians were not even familiar with the disease, and some even challenged the validity of the report.

I was finally able to obtain the information I needed at the James A. Baker Institute for Animal Health at Cornell University. Two of their researchers had been working on the disease and had been successful in isolating the virus. They were calling it canine parvovirus.

The virus caused lesions in a dog's intestines identical to those found in a cat's intestines from the feline distemper virus. With that clue, the viruses were compared and found to be serologically identical. This was the breakthrough the researchers needed.

The reasoning was this: If the feline distemper virus was identical to the virus that was causing parvovirus in dogs, it was conceivable that the feline distemper vaccine, given to dogs, could prevent parvovirus.

The theory was tested at the Baker Institute by giving a limited population of dogs two doses of killed virus feline distemper vaccine several days apart and then exposing the dogs to the parvovirus. Another group of dogs were not given the vaccine but were also exposed to the parvovirus.

Every unvaccinated dog became ill, but not one of the vaccinated dogs contracted the disease or became ill from the vaccine. The researchers felt certain they had at least a short-term solution.

Still, there were a lot of questions to answer about the virus before anyone could feel safe. Other viruses usually die in a matter of minutes when shed from their host. Not the canine parvovirus. This one was a new and frighteningly different virus. It defied temperature extremes, surviving for months, and maybe even years, away from its host, in freezing temperatures as well as in torrid heat. Not one of the known bactericidals or virucidals used for cleaning in animal shelters was found to kill the virus. Oddly enough, the one cleaning agent that did prove lethal was common household bleach. The formula was one part bleach to thirty parts water. We were extremely fortunate that our automatic metering devices could be used to feed this bleach solution into our high-pressure sanitizing system. We considered the cost insignificant when compared to what might result from an outbreak of the disease.

Theories on how this new virus might have developed began to proliferate. The most fascinating one was that some researcher, while cultivating a feline distemper vaccine, used a dog's blood instead of a cat's, and through a quirk of fate, the new mutant virus was formed. Fortunately, the virus affected only dogs and was harmless to cats, other animals, and humans.

The solution for combating this threatening disease seemed simple, but there is nothing simple about the human mind and its propensity for creating problems. Feline distemper vaccine was approved by the Food and Drug Administration only for use on cats. Even though millions of doses had been administered to cats, it had never been clinically tested on dogs. The limited testing of the Baker Institute for Animal Health was not adequate to discern any long-term results. Only time could do this, and we didn't have the time.

In less than six months from the day it was discovered, outbreaks of parvovirus were reported in England, northern Europe, Australia, and in every one of the United States, including Alaska. Over the next few weeks, I received calls from kennel operators all over the country reporting massive outbreaks of canine parvovirus, with horrible loss of animal life. One facility lost over one hundred dogs, while another one reported eighty-five dead. The stories kept coming in from every region of the country. No place was safe.

Researchers began referring to the disease as the Legionnaire's disease of dogs.

Dr. Mahr and I continued exchanging information, and after due consideration decided we would both require every dog coming in for boarding to be vaccinated with two injections of feline distemper vaccine given ten days apart. If the owners refused, we would not board their dogs. We advised other kennel owners of our decision, but only a few were willing to go along with us. The others felt they would wait until they experienced an outbreak before taking action.

The task of convincing our customers that they should have their dogs vaccinated with a vaccine approved only for cats was not going to be easy. We decided the best way to do it was to print a pamphlet and mail it to each dog owner.

To eliminate any conflict with the local veterinary association, I employed Dr. David Epstein, a local veterinarian, to contact the Baker Institute and obtain all the necessary information from Drs. Leland Carmichael and Roy Pollack, the two veterinarians responsible for most of the parvovirus research. Dr. Epstein had good credentials, and in addition to operating his own veterinary hospital, has a weekly radio program that deals with animal health matters.

Over 15,000 pamphlets, titled "A Killer Is Stalking Your Dog," were printed and mailed to our customers. In addition, a copy with a cover letter was sent to every veterinarian in the greater Chicago area.

Although some of the veterinarians discarded the literature without reading it, many more began calling and requesting additional information. Customers asked for additional copies to mail to relatives who owned dogs in other states. Pet shops and kennels from all over the country requested, and were granted permission, to reproduce it. There is no way of telling how many dog owners read this pamphlet, but we received mail from as far away as Thailand.

As news of increased outbreaks was received, we decided to send a copy of the pamphlet together with a press release to the major wire services. Public awareness of the disease was still lacking, and neither the

133

newspapers nor public broadcasting services had issued any warnings.

All three major wire services indicated interest in the story. If true, it was a spectacular news item, a possibly mutant killer virus that appeared mysteriously and could result in the death of a dog in less than twenty-four hours. Naturally, its authenticity had to be verified before the story could be released. Regrettably, the news media did not check with the Baker Institute. Instead, they called the Chicago Veterinary Medical Association.

Despite all of the evidence at their disposal, the CVMA assured the news services that there was no imminent threat, and that parvovirus was just a minor inconvenience that would soon pass.

Only one Chicago newspaper mentioned the disease. Under the heading, "Scare Tactic or Epidemic?" the *Chicago Sun Times* printed the responses of several veterinarians to our pamphlet.

A spokesman for the CVMA ridiculed our assertions and was quoted as saying that "No one will stand by the vaccine." This same veterinarian went on to state that he was, however, administering the feline distemper vaccine to show dogs. Another veterinarian who operated a large boarding kennel in Des Plaines, Illinois, also advised against using the feline distemper vaccine, although he conceded to the reporter that he was vaccinating every dog that boarded at his kennel!

The reaction of our adversaries in the Chicago Veterinary Medical Association was to urge their fellow members to begin a boycott of American Pet Motels.

A boycott wasn't enough for some of the members. They embarked on an organized letter-writing campaign. State veterinary associations, national veterinary associations, the Department of Agriculture, and various national veterinary journals all received letters protesting our pamphlet's distribution. If these other organizations thought we were out of line, not one contacted us to say so. We did hear from some of them, but not for the purpose our adversaries intended.

"DVM, The Newsletter of Veterinary Medicine," conducted a telephone interview with us and with the CVMA. In the July 1979 edition of the magazine, they published a very fair and unbiased review of the interviews. The CVMA again went on record stating that I was using scare tactics and trying to tell veterinarians what vaccines to use. "We think the danger is being overemphasized," their spokesman proclaimed.

Ironically, on the front page of this very same publication, the main headline stated in bold black print, **"Canine Parvovirus Diagnosed in All 50 States; Linked to FPL."**

An article in *Time* magazine reported an estimated 1,500 dogs dead of parvovirus in the Minneapolis–St. Paul area alone; 124 deaths in South Florida; 1,000 deaths in Corpus Christi. In Seattle, Washington, an epidemic forced the city to close its animal shelter. Serological studies in New York and Washington showed that 25 percent of household dogs tested had evidence of previous infection. In Washington, D.C., New Jersey, and Georgia, the figure was 50 percent. If the CVMA was correct, the rest of the world was wrong.

I mentioned that one of our pamphlets found its way to Bangkok, Thailand, where almost a hundred dogs had died with symptoms of parvovirus. Due to our pamphlet, they began a general inoculation of the dog population with feline distemper vaccine, and the outbreak was immediately brought under control.

Major newspapers, including *The Wall Street Journal,* printed daily reports of growing outbreaks and deaths from parvovirus, but still the CVMA assured Chicago's dog owners and their own members that it was nothing to be concerned about.

The disease did not bypass Chicago and its suburbs. Almost four hundred beagles at the Argonne National Laboratory, on the outskirts of Chicago, became infected. Willy Neckers, a kennel that had operated since World War I, had to close due to an outbreak. They never reopened. From Hinsdale to the shores of Lake Michigan, outbreaks of parvovirus were reported. Dogs living in high-rises along Chicago's swank million-dollar mile were not spared, although some had never been out of their apartments. Unfortunately, the disease also struck the Anti-Cruelty Society, in the heart of Chicago, and resulted in an unspecified number of deaths, as well as the closing of the shelter.

One member of the letter-writing campaign group,

who also operated a veterinary hospital and boarding kennel in Glencoe, felt so strongly about the issue that he wrote assuring me that if I kept our facilities as clean as he did, I would not have to worry about parvovirus. Obviously this professional had never visited our kennels or read the literature. The Argonne National Laboratory was anything but a pig sty and they had four hundred cases of parvovirus.

While responsible veterinarians all over the country were advising their clients to have their dogs vaccinated with the killed virus feline distemper vaccine, in Chicago, many dog owners were told that the vaccine was worthless and in some cases, that it could kill their dog.

At the height of the problem, spokesmen for the CVMA distorted the statements of the Baker Research Institute to convince their membership that the vaccine was ineffective and possibly dangerous. Their persuasive argument was that ". . . even Dr. Carmichael, the head researcher at the Baker Institute, would not recommend the use of feline distemper vaccine for dogs. . . ."

It was a cleverly worded distortion.

What Dr. Carmichael said was that ". . . as a research scientist, it would be a violation of federal law to recommend, across state lines, the use of a drug for dogs that the FDA had approved only for cats."

He also said, "Experiments in our laboratory have shown, however, that two doses of commercial inactivated Feline Panleukopenia vaccine given two weeks apart, provided protection against the canine parvovirus."

The entire disagreement hinged on whether parvovirus was a real threat to the area's canine population or not, and I felt the continuing hostility would not bring about a valid conclusion. I wanted to end it, and I was willing to revise my actions according to the results of an impartial survey.

I telephoned the CVMA and suggested that they conduct a survey of the area's veterinarians to find out how many dogs with symptoms of parvovirus they were treating each month. I was told that such a survey would be much too expensive to conduct.

I then made them an offer in genuine good faith. I told them that American Pet Motels would pay for the printing, mailing, and tabulation of the survey, but the CVMA could have total control of the survey and its results. I even agreed never to acknowledge that our company paid for the survey.

"It would still be too expensive. We just can't do it," I was told. There was just no interest among this group to determine the dimensions of the problem.

The CVMA boycott did hurt our business, but the real damage was the needless suffering and widespread loss of life among the canine population in Illinois. Our requirement of feline distemper vaccinations, the use of bleach in our sanitizing system, and the prompt treatment of any suspicious symptoms permitted us to get through the epidemic with just a single incident, and fortunately, it had a happy conclusion.

Several days after she had picked up her dog, the owner of Oliver, an often boarded, Old English sheepdog, telephoned and reported that Oliver was in a hospital with parvovirus.

I knew Oliver well. He was one of those huge, shaggy bundles of energy that constantly demonstrated an adolescent disdain for obedience and an insatiable appetite for love and affection.

Now, he lay on a table with IV needles stuck in his veins and disgorging huge quantities of blood. There was no doubt about the symptoms and less doubt about the eventual outcome.

Although the disease may have been contracted after the dog left our motel, I still told the owner that we would cover all her veterinary treatment up to our two-hundred-and-fifty-dollar limit.

Several days later, Oliver's owner called to tell me that Oliver was still ill, but that the bill was now over three hundred dollars and she could not afford to continue treatment. She was going to have Oliver euthanized.

One of the benefits of being in charge is the power to break rules. It is a virtue for those rare occasions when the book says one thing and your heart tells you something else.

I told the woman not to do it. As long as there was

the slightest chance that Oliver could recover, APM would pick up the bill.

Oliver remained in a comatose condition for several more weeks, receiving huge quantities of intravenous fluids and being pumped full of antibiotics. Still, he clung to life with a tenacious grip.

Finally, his veterinarian called us. Oliver was on his way back. In a few days he would be going home.

We paid the entire bill. Bad business judgment, perhaps, but the only way for me. I have learned to argue the justification of such actions by insisting that the welfare of the pet must at least equal any other priority of our business.

# 17

# GROOMING FOR HEALTH

When I told people of how I lost my ocelot, I began to hear more and more stories of other people whose pets had been injured or strangled by being snared by their collars. As a result, we made it a fast and firm rule that no boarding animal would be allowed to wear a collar, choker, or harness while staying with us.

The wisdom of this policy was demonstrated again recently when I took in a year-old Eskimo spitz with long, bushy white hair. As the owner removed the leather collar, from habit, I ran my fingers over the neck area for a choker. I felt two ridges of skin, but when I probed deeper, I found a tight leather choke collar buried in the folds of the flesh.

The owner was surprised and embarrassed. This collar had been placed on the dog when it was still a puppy and had been completely forgotten. Now, as the dog approached full size, the collar was almost completely hidden within the fleshy folds of its neck. We were able to remove it by cutting it with a special pair of clippers we keep available for just such occasions, as this was not the first time something like this occurred.

Before entering this business, I was as ignorant about the subject of dog grooming as the majority of dog owners still are. I presumed grooming was something that was done more for the satisfaction of the owner than for the health of the dog. For show dogs, it was a process of cutting and brushing the hair into weird and grotesque styles.

But dog and cat grooming is far more than a cosmetic exercise, and in some cases it turns out to be a matter of life or death. Proper bathing and grooming of dogs and cats is much more necessary than most pet owners suspect. In fact, the lack of grooming can sometimes mean a life of pain and torment for a dog or cat, and I suspect more than one poor pet has been put to sleep because the owners thought it was vicious when in fact it was merely a victim of its owner's benign neglect.

Over the years, our groomers have removed fish hooks, needles, pieces of barbed wire, and a host of other foreign objects that they found embedded in the bodies of the dogs they were grooming. Infections, tumors, growths, and numerous skin problems, not even suspected by the owners, are frequently found during the grooming process. Few owners really give their pet's body the thorough going over that a qualified groomer will. Most often, the owner's inspection is limited to a pat on the head or a few strokes on the back.

On one occasion, a groomer found a metal choke chain embedded underneath the skin of a dog's neck. The choker had been placed on the dog while it was a puppy. As he grew, the chain cut into the dog's neck and its new flesh actually grew around it. This case required veterinary surgery.

Every week, we find dewclaws that have grown completely around and into the fleshy part of a dog's feet. A dog that runs on concrete will wear his nails down. But today, most dogs are raised in a carpeted house, and their nails will continue to grow until they are cut by someone or they finally curve around and grow into the flesh. I have seen dogs whose legs were actually misshapen because the length of their toenails interfered with their gait. When their nails reach such a length, it is virtually impossible for a groomer to clip them. The dog must be taken to a veterinarian and anesthetized to spare the poor animal the pain.

Short-haired dogs may need only an occasional bath and brushing, but long-haired dogs require frequent brushings. Dogs shed their hair and grow a new coat each season. I've heard owners threaten to have their dogs put to sleep because their hair is getting all over the carpets and furniture. The truth of the matter is that the fault lies with the pet owners. If they would take the proper type of brush and comb and use it a few times each week, they and their pets would be a lot happier and healthier.

Sometimes a dog will come into the pet motel with such a fetid smell that you wonder how the owner tolerated it in his home. The worst cases are those in which the dog can barely move because its hair is knotted together in one massive tangle. Even the eyes are sometimes stuck closed due to the accumulation of dirt and discharge around them. Every grooming parlor in the country has experienced cases so bad that they have to refer the owner to a veterinarian where the pet can be shaved while under an anesthetic.

All too often, the removal of this matted hair will reveal large sections of raw flesh, the result of air being unable to dry the skin, which actually rots away. The owners are usually unaware of the condition because they never groom the pet themselves, nor do they have a professional groomer do it. Yet an excellent slicker brush and a proper comb can be purchased in any pet shop for only a few dollars. It should be a requirement of pet ownership.

The wisdom of grooming was never more emphatically impressed on me than by an incident that occurred in our own pet motel.

The lesson for one family began when they brought in two Lhasa apsos for boarding. Jason was neatly brushed, with the hair over his eyes tied out of the way with a small plastic barrette. The other dog, Molly, was a basket case. Her hair was badly matted and the odor that emanated from her was noticeable from across the room. The owners were quite conscious of Molly's condition and kept apologizing that there was nothing they could do because she had such a bad disposition. She would snap or bite anyone who tried to brush or even touch her. She not only bit strangers, they said, but she also bit them, and while they stood there, the family debated the wisdom of putting the dog to sleep.

I shuddered when I heard the receptionist automatically ask if they would like to have both dogs bathed or groomed and the owners agreed. Knowing the attitudes of our groomers, developed over several years of being snapped at and often bitten, I doubted if any one of them would touch Molly.

The dogs were boarded together in an Imperial suite, which I passed by several times each day. One of life's greatest pleasures for me is to go into each room and spend a little time playing with the occupants. Heartbreak was when a dog wouldn't let me. Molly was such a one.

She and Jason would be lying on the bed together, and when I approached, Jason would jump up and squeal with excitement. He loved to have me brush him, and he'd climb into my lap and run his tongue all over my face in an enthusiastic display of affection.

Molly was not so inclined. She would crouch in the far corner of the bed and growl continuously. The slightest move toward her resulted in her snapping and trying to bite me.

Usually we groom a dog on the day it is going home so it is nice and neat for the occasion. Perhaps because she felt she would have a lot of trouble with Molly, Karen, the manager of the grooming shop, decided to do it only a few days after the dog had arrived.

Knowing Karen's reluctance to groom problem dogs, I can only presume that it was another act of divine providence that she even attempted the feat. In the several years that Karen had been grooming, she had never been bitten, a claim few groomers can make. Of course, as manager, she could choose which dogs she would groom, but the minute a dog proved uncooperative, she simply put it back in its room and refused to groom it. More than one recalcitrant dog went home only partially groomed. Although our receptionist had meant well, I was confident that none of our groomers, least of all Karen, would groom Molly.

Then, one morning when I was ringing in the previous day's grooming charges, I was surprised to find a charge for Molly. I couldn't believe it. I opened the sliding glass door to the grooming parlor and asked Karen if she had the correct dog's name on the charge slip. She laughed as she nodded. Yes, she knew exactly what I meant.

Apparently, with the help of another groomer and a leather muzzle, Karen had managed to shave the dog and remove the matted entanglements. I found it hard to believe her when she told me that once she had Molly half shaved, the dog had ceased its struggling and biting, and had actually let Karen finish her with only minor objections.

After work that day, I went to Molly's room and looked in. There was Jason, just as presentable as the day he came in. Next to him lay Molly, looking like a plucked chicken. Her skin was covered with small sores and glowed almost pink.

As soon as I entered the room, Jason jumped off the bed and began begging me to pick him up. I had just knelt down and let him climb into my lap when Molly jumped off the bed and also came to me. I reached down cautiously and began patting her head. Her long naked tail, with a little pompom at the end, began swinging back and forth wildly, and her legs began pawing at the air in an attempt to climb into my lap. I helped her up, and the two dogs reached for my face with their little tongues darting in and out of their mouths. Apprehension gave way to laughter as the three of us became good friends.

Molly was not a vicious dog. She was merely a victim of benign neglect. Probably at some time she had been permitted to get dirty and, as her hair became matted, her movements became painful. Each time she moved or someone picked her up, it was like somebody pulling her hair. In pain, the dog responded in the only way she knew how. She tried to protect herself by biting. The longer the condition continued, the more dirt her hair collected, until finally, the hair in front of her eyes no longer reflected the light necessary for her to distinguish friend from foe. All she saw was shadows, and each shadow was a threat of pain.

The matting problem is far from unique to dogs. Long-haired cats, such as Persians and Himalayans, also require frequent brushing, or they can suffer the same painful experiences.

Another problem, more common in the South, is that of fleas.

In a Florida pet motel, I saw bathing tubs run red with blood from dogs whose skins had been perforated by thousands of fleas. So completely had they been infested that the groomer had to remove huge nests from the dogs' ears and even from under the eyelids. In some cases, the dogs had been bled to the extent that their gums were almost white, indicating a severe anemic condition. There are recorded cases of pets dying of anemia caused by fleas.

When we were interested in a small kennel in Sarasota, Florida, everyone told us that flea infestation was a fact of life. Some boarding facilities even required every boarding pet to be dipped first in a bath of chemical flea killer. Even so, there was no guarantee that your pet still wouldn't go home with fleas. Kennel owners in the South are not joking when they state that animals receiving flea and tick baths are guaranteed to be free of fleas only up to their front door. All guarantees end there.

We refused to accept that this was how it had to be. We felt that checking pets when they came in and bathing those with fleas, daily sterilization of the animal quarters with a high-pressure sanitizing system, and regular treatment of the grounds and facilities would make it possible to guarantee that if a pet came in without fleas, it would go home without fleas. We give that guarantee in Chicago and we became the only ones to give it in Florida.

When we took over the Sarasota facility, it was alive with vermin. Cockroaches, fleas, ants—you name it and this kennel had it. We couldn't even turn out the kennel lights at night because the dog runs would suddenly become alive with roaches. In the mornings, the carpets would be shredded and the kennel would look as if a hurricane had hit it, the result of some of the dogs trying to kill the roaches.

We began a program of fumigating and spraying that continued for three full months. After that, it became a regular maintenance item. Not only did we eliminate the vermin problem, but in the four years that we operated the kennel, we had only two complaints of pets going home with fleas, and both of those cases had questionable aspects.

For those who think grooming is unpleasant for the dog, I wish they could be in the lobby when Fred Chase, a large standard poodle, is brought in for his six-week grooming. His owner has only to drop his leash and Fred will bound into the grooming parlor and jump on Karen's table. If he finds all the tables occupied, he will gallop into the bathing room and jump into one of the bathtubs. This dog enjoys grooming so much he has memorized the entire procedure and holds out his paws in the proper sequence to be clipped, without even being told.

While many health problems can be avoided by regular grooming, I can think of at least one time when it created a health hazard—for an owner, not a dog.

A neatly dressed man entered the pet motel one Saturday and asked to have his dog completely shaved. The dog was a beautiful, black standard poodle with a long, handsome coat meticulously trimmed in a show cut.

When I heard the man request the dog be stripped, I was certain he was making a mistake and questioned him. No, the man assured us. He knew exactly what the term implied, and he wanted the dog shaved completely bare.

I still thought it was a bad decision and suggested that maybe it would be better just to trim the dog or maybe put it into a puppy cut so it would still have some hair covering its body.

The man was adamant. He wanted the dog shaved as smooth as a billiard ball.

I sensed something was wrong, but you soon learn that when you're dealing with pet owners, nothing is bizarre. I watched Karen lead the dog into the grooming parlor and instruct one of the groomers to strip it.

Just before noon, a very smartly dressed lady called for the dog. She was wearing an expensively tailored suit, and her fingers sported several large diamond rings.

As Karen led the dog from the grooming parlor, the lady quietly remarked, "You've got the wrong dog. That's not my dog."

145

We assured her it was.

Her face turned ashen. "Oh, my God!" she shrieked. "What have you done? That's a champion show dog. How could you! I'm supposed to fly her to New York in two hours for the International Dog Show. How could you? How could you?"

Karen and I looked at each other and then at the dog. It really looked like an oversized plucked goose. I could guarantee her it certainly wasn't going to win any prizes with that haircut. I don't think they would have even allowed the dog on a beach looking as it did.

I pulled the grooming card and read her the exact instructions her husband had given us. I had written down every word, fearing that some problem might arise.

When I finished, the lady just stood there. Then, quietly, she apologized for her outburst and explained the strange situation. She was heavily involved in showing her prized dog all over the country, and as her travels increased, so did her husband's objections. When this particular show came up, his resentment precipitated an intense argument between the two.

That fateful morning, she made the mistake of asking her husband to take the dog to our grooming parlor to be bathed and brushed out. When he stalked out of the house, she never dreamed what he had in mind to resolve the problem. It would be some months before she traveled again.

# THE GERIATRIC TRADE

A surprising part of our increasing business came from an unexpected source—old and ill dogs and cats. The illnesses were not contagious diseases, but were associated with heredity and advanced aging.

There is an increased hazard in boarding old animals. Our canine and feline senior citizens are the most likely to suffer kidney failure due to stress. Once uremic poisoning begins in their system, it is virtually irreversible.

Because of our reputation, more and more veterinarians began referring these clients to us. Blind animals, deaf animals, cardiac cases, epileptics, and diabetics began coming to us with increasing regularity. Some veterinarians referred them because they knew we would furnish the extra care required. Others had a different motive.

Some of the animals should never have been admitted, but not all of the problems were obvious. We were so used to seeing owners coddling their pets that we did not think it unusual when they insisted on carrying their dogs to their rooms. Only after the pet owners left would we realize that the dogs could not walk or even stand up.

Each day, these dogs had to be lifted into a bathtub and bathed because they couldn't control their body functions and soiled themselves continuously. Others had to be hand fed or required frequent veterinary attention. In one case, an old St. Bernard was actually restored to life by our kennel master's application of mouth-to-mouth resuscitation.

All of our "senior citizens" received a disproportionate share of the staff's attention, but sick and injured pets also added new emotional demands on all of us that were unfair. More than once I found an attendant sitting with one of them, crying, because of the animal's plight. They belonged in a hospital, not in a boarding facility.

To resolve the problem, we finally initiated a new policy. All dogs had to be able to walk to their rooms.

You'd be surprised at the ingenious ploys some pet owners devised to get their dogs past the reception desk. Some openly exhorted their dogs to make a valiant effort to walk the distance. One of the saddest scenes was watching an owner urging on his dysplastic German shepherd. The poor animal would pull itself up and with the first step, as his hips gave way to the weight of his body, he'd fall over and over again.

Because so many of these older guests required special care and unanticipated veterinary attention, I was constantly being pressured not to accept older pets, but I refused to give in. Again, the reason was strictly personal. I knew the kind of care these pets would get in some boarding facilities, and I knew the kind of care they would receive from us. I always felt they had a better chance with us, and they deserved at least this.

The policy is sometimes unrewarding. In one case, a diabetic dog had to receive insulin injections every evening at eight o'clock. When injections are required, I permit only the director of animal welfare or myself to administer them. I was the one giving the injections to this dog.

Everything went well until the day the dog was picked up by its owner. For some reason he had not eaten his food that morning, and the owner was so advised.

The next day, the owner telephoned and told me that her dog was in the hospital and might not survive. She was irate because her veterinarian had told her that his tests indicated the dog had not received its scheduled insulin injection. Her veterinarian was wrong. I was sure the dog had received its insulin because I was the one who had administered it.

The veterinarian neglected to tell the lady that the stress of being reunited with its owner, the body temperature, plus any number of other factors could account for this condition. We paid the veterinarian's charges for treating the dog until it was stabilized again, but the owner remained displeased, believing we had not administered the injection.

A very common condition among elderly dogs is blindness. Most dogs develop cataracts in their advanced years, and while these can be removed in many cases, the cost of surgery prevents many owners from having it done.

Surprisingly, blindness has not been the problem we anticipated. Dogs apparently adapt to the hardship by utilizing other sensory organs to a higher degree. Given only a few minutes in their room, most blind dogs are able to find their way to their outside runs and to return at will. They find their water bowls and food without help and maneuver in and out of their beds without assistance. I never cease to be amazed that I can place a cookie anyplace in the room and the dog will go to that spot and retrieve it. Instead of being a burden, most of these dogs are better boarders than their healthier counterparts because their appetites appear also to have improved. I do not recall a single instance when we have had a problem getting a blind dog to eat our regular diets.

There have been some unusual incidents, but the one I remember best was the time a huge Great Dane was boarded with a twenty-two-year-old blind and deaf miniature poodle.

It was literally impossible for the poodle to move without the Great Dane following it. The enormous Dane would hover over the poodle, permitting it to move freely until it approached some obstacle. Then, the Dane would intercede with its head and deflect the poodle in another direction.

When you entered the room and approached the poodle, the Dane would step forward and stare directly into your eyes. When you held the poodle's head to administer eye drops, the Dane would not interfere, but just stood there, as if poised to strike should you make one harmful gesture toward his friend. He would guide the poodle to its food and water, but never drink or eat himself until his friend had had its fill. I have witnessed hundreds of similar examples of unusual devotion by one animal to another. People hearing these stories tell similar stories of their own, yet still they ask if I believe animals can think or reason. If they cannot, I defy anyone to explain what I have seen and experienced in this business.

Call your travel agent for reservations or take out a suitcase, and observe the change in your dog or cat. I've heard of cats and dogs hiding till their owners missed their planes. One veterinarian told me of a case where a German shepherd walked into its master's bedroom, where they were packing their suitcases for a trip. The dog took one look at the suitcases and leapt out the second-story window. It didn't work. The owners still went on their vacation while the dog recovered from a broken leg in the veterinarian's hospital. The veterinarian thinks the dog attempted suicide.

Many pets actually seem to enjoy the boarding experience. Some apparently do not. We have been told by some owners that when their pets go home, they behave in strange ways. Some will totally ignore the owner, while others will hide under a couch or bed, making the owner feel guilty. I have heard of several instances where the pet went home and deliberately eliminated on its master's bed. Pets have a variety of ways to convey their feelings.

One of the more humorous cases involved a small terrier mutt that was shipped to us from Japan. The dog boarded excellently while the owner got relocated in the Chicago area. When the owner called for it, the dog, as soon as it started down the corridor and saw its owner, held its left paw up and limped to where the owner was standing.

The owner showered the dog with affection and concern, but none of us could find the cause of the limping. In accord with our policy, I suggested he take the dog to a veterinarian to find out why the dog was limping, and, if there was any problem, to have it corrected and send us the bill.

X-rays and a thorough examination failed to reveal

any problem, and the following day the dog was bouncing all over his new home as if nothing had ever been wrong. We paid almost sixty dollars in veterinary bills.

About a month later, we were called upon to board this little dog again for another two weeks. When the owner called for the dog this time, his pet came down the corridor limping again, but holding his right foot in the air this time.

The owner took one look at the dog and publicly admonished him. "Scooter, you ol' faker. Put that paw down and behave yourself!"

Right away, the dog lowered his head and followed his master outside on all four paws. This dog was one of many con artists who know how to extract the last measure of sympathy and attention from their masters.

Because of the growing number of pets that were being put on all kinds of vitamins and useless supplements, we finally initiated a modest charge for the administration of any kind of pill or medication. Most pet owners are happy to pay this extra charge in exchange for the knowledge their pet will receive the medication. The additional charge has helped reduce the number of requests for unnecessary supplements. Unfortunately, there have been a few instances where a pet owner did not tell us that their animal required medication for a serious illness in order to save the fifty-cent charge. In at least one case, there was no doubt that it caused the dog's death. At other times, when symptoms developed, we are able to check with the pet's veterinarian. If the veterinarian feels it is important, we will have our driver pick up the medication, and we will administer it. As a result, we have a large box filled with the unused portions of medications. It is not uncommon for these owners to refuse to pay either for the medicine or for its administration when they pick up their pets.

It is very important for a pet owner to advise a boarding facility about any illnesses or problems their pets have incurred. If they don't, it is easy not to notice certain symptoms until there is blood or some other obvious sign. A pet owner could be wagering his pet's life against the few pennies it would cost to have the medicine administered as prescribed.

Some people will conceal an illness out of fear that

we will not accept their pet. In the vast majority of cases, this will not happen. The only time we refuse a pet with medical problems is if it has a contagious illness or if we consider the pet's condition so poor that we cannot properly care for it. Heart trouble, epilepsy, kidney stones, and dozens of other problems are sometimes left for us to find out about on our own, and this means the loss of valuable time during which a needless examination is made to diagnose the problem. When the problem is finally established, additional time is lost in obtaining treatment from the owner's veterinarian. The wasted time could be critical for the animal.

Some pet owners are just naturally suspicious, and no matter what you tell them, they choose to believe something else.

I remember getting a telephone call from a man who complained that his dog barked incessantly, and he wanted to know what he could do to silence him. The only thing I could recommend was for the man to have the dog obedience trained.

The man was not satisfied with that answer. He wanted to know what drugs or tranquilizers he could use. I assured him that drugs were not the answer. Besides being expensive and dangerous, they would have only a short-term effect. The dog would probably return to barking as soon as the drugs wore off.

"Well, what drugs do you use in your pet motel?" the man demanded to know. "You must get a lot of barkers in there."

"Very rarely," I answered. "The dogs do bark when it's feeding time or when we're taking dogs in or out of the kennel, but as a rule, even the worst barker will settle down after a short time."

Nothing I said seemed to satisfy the caller. Finally, I suggested he contact his veterinarian. There is one method, a surgical procedure that involves severing the vocal chords of the dog. It was the only absolute resolution I knew of, but one that I was reluctant even to suggest to the caller.

Finally, convinced that I had no magical solution, the man confessed the real reason for his questions. His dog had boarded with us and when it returned home, it merely lay around the house and didn't bark at anything. The man said that prior to boarding, his dog was an obnoxious barker who would be provoked by anything and everything. He was almost intolerable. After returning home from being boarded, the dog was a completely different animal. Nothing seemed to bother him and he had stopped his obnoxious barking.

I wish I did know a secret to stop certain dogs from barking. I'd bottle it and make a million dollars.

One owner had a different way of presenting her complaint. She had been waiting in the lobby for her dog to be brought from the kennels. Every few minutes, she would interrupt the receptionist, seeking to be reassured that her dog had been receiving its special food and medication. No matter how many times she was told that it had, she still seemed to harbor some doubts.

When the attendant finally arrived, the lady scooped the dog up in her arms and hurried from the building. A few minutes later, she came pushing her way back through the crowd at the front desk, holding the dog backward under her right arm.

Lifting its tail up with her left hand, she thrust the dog's backside into my face.

"Look!" she yelled at me. "Look at that!"

I stood there speechless, gazing into this dog's rear end, for what purpose I didn't know, while dozens of onlookers stood by in bewilderment.

My first urge was to reply, "Yes, there's another one," but diplomacy forbade such a response. Before I could think of something to say, the lady withdrew the dog without another word and left the building. I still am not sure of what she was talking about, but I suspect it had something to do with an anal gland problem. However, to achieve an amicable resolution of any kind of complaint, I strongly urge pet owners to approach the kennel operator face to face.

I am sure that most pet owners worry about boarding their pets, but some are almost paranoid. You can satisfy most, but a few you never can. The astounding thing is that the ones who complain the most will continue to come back over and over again, finding something to complain about each time, of course.

They will moan about the hours, groan about the service, complain about the charges, but they'll keep coming back. Some customers are so unreasonable and unpleasant that even our employees argue that their pets should not be allowed to board with us anymore. But, I insist that we continue to serve them. I do it because I don't believe their pets could get equal treatment in most of the other kennels, and that's the real reason we are in business—for the pets, not for their owners.

At least one pet owner had to learn the hard way. The first time she boarded her Old English sheepdog with us, it broke out with canine cough shortly after it went home. The lady claimed that the virus was due to our lack of proper care and insisted that we should refund all of her boarding and grooming charges in addition to paying her veterinary bill.

When we declined to refund the boarding and grooming charges, she contacted the Better Business Bureau and the Department of Agriculture, and wrote in to the consumer action column of the *Chicago Tribune*, claiming that we were disreputable and irresponsible and should be forced out of business. After we responded to inquiries from all these sources, none elected to pursue the matter.

About two years later, I received a personal telephone call from this same lady. She was extremely apologetic and obviously embarrassed. She didn't have to remind me, but she mentioned the occasion of her first boarding and its subsequent consequences.

"Mr. Leeds," she admitted, "I know now that what happened had nothing to do with the pet motel. Since boarding with you, I have boarded my dog with several kennels and even with my veterinarian. You can't imagine the problems I've had. I want to come back. I'm sorry for what happened and I promise I won't cause you any trouble if you will just board my dog. Quite honestly, if I can't board him with you, I would not board him with anyone."

I neither needed nor wanted any such assurances. I was delighted to have another chance to prove to this pet owner that we were every bit as good as we claimed.

No matter how good any boarding facility is, problems will always occur that are beyond its control. Heaven knows a kennel has enough problems; they shouldn't be blamed for those they can't help. A dog tries to dig through the concrete floor and goes home with the pads of its feet covered with sores. Or, in the middle of the night, a dog tries to chew a hole in its specially constructed chain link enclosure and breaks a tooth or lacerates its mouth. There are dogs that are bought in already carrying the canine cough virus, but the infection has not matured to the point where the symptoms are noticeable. Even the pet owner doesn't know his dog is a carrier, and by the time the symptoms are obvious, half a dozen other dogs have been infected. These are the types of problems over which a kennel has no control.

We have found, also, that it is virtually impossible to predetermine how a pet will behave when it is boarded. The results may be totally different from one time to another. The vast majority of pets board well and go home in as good or better condition than when they entered the kennel. A very, very small number of pets and owners cause 100 percent of the problems.

We regularly board the attack-trained dogs of several nearby cities' police departments. Even though these dogs are highly stressed and wholly unapproachable when they are with their handlers, they board well, like most other dogs, when they are left by themselves in our kennels.

I doubt that pets are much different from people, and I haven't met many people who didn't need a few days to recuperate after their vacations. I'd guess that 99 percent of the pets go home after the vacation period in better shape than their masters. But, for the other 1 percent, boarding was a "trying" experience: trying to out-yodel every dog in the kennel; trying to jump on every pet and person passing by; trying to bark at every little noise, day and night, neglecting their sleep and keeping others from theirs; trying to do everything but rest.

The continuous mellow music in all of our animal facilities does have a pacifying effect, but there is always one troubadour beagle or basset hound who thinks it's a sing-along and he'll try harder.

Yes, for some, boarding is a very "trying" experience. Many of the compensations and rewards of this business do not show on the financial statement. They occur each time some elderly pet owner steps up to the counter and says, "My name is such and such. I boarded my little dog Fido here. Is he still alive?"

It is now such a familiar routine that we automatically break into a grin.

"Why, certainly," we reply. "In fact, he was just asking about you this morning."

Then, you watch her face as her dog comes charging down the long corridor from the kennels and climbs into her arms for a tearful reunion. That moment is the highest reward a good kennel can earn.

# 19

# SOMEDAY YOUR "PRINCE" WILL COME

It is impossible for a dog owner to stand in our lobby for any length of time with his pets before another owner will engage him in a discussion of what kind of dog makes the best pet.

This never seems to happen to cat owners. Possibly it is because cat owners already know the breed they own is the best, although one cat lover insists it is because cat lovers love all cats!

But, if there were a thousand different breeds and you asked a thousand different dog owners, you would receive as many different replies.

There is a different dog for each of us. Of the many guests I've had the opportunity of knowing, there are two breeds whose owners seldom report a fault; the golden retriever, in the large dog class, and the West Highland terrier, in the small dog class. Each of these breeds is well behaved and possesses a limitless reservoir of love, loyalty, and devotion. I have found them to be the most social of all breeds. They get along excellently with children, and they welcome attention from anyone.

It is wrong to categorize any particular breed as bad. I have seen vicious Dobermans and pit bulls, as well as vicious Pekingese and Chihuahuas, but an ill-natured dog is an exception to its breed. There are some bad dogs of every breed.

Like other people in this business, I find it reasonable to recommend a small dog for a small home and a large dog for a home with a lot of space. It is logical to assume that large dogs like Irish setters and German shepherds need more space to exercise in than a Chihuahua or a terrier. It seems reasonable to assume this, but it's not necessarily the case.

Every breed of dog has been raised in the confines of research kennels, and they have lived full and normal life expectancies. Experience with many thousands of pet owners has shown me that a St. Bernard can grow up in a two-room apartment and attain all the health and happiness loving care can provide, just as well as any toy breed. And, of course, I have not found small breeds deficient just because they were raised in huge open spaces.

We have boarded numerous large dogs, even Irish wolfhounds and Great Danes, who lived with their owners in small apartment units and were always healthy and appeared normal. It isn't the quantity but the quality of space that counts.

I have a theory about pets. I don't believe most people actually choose their pets; I believe the opposite. Most pets choose their owners. It's a confirming act of divine intervention that often the person who swears he would never own a cat ultimately ends up with one, and the person who hasn't the slightest desire to be the owner of a dog ends up with two or three. It is as if some dimension of life is not complete without them.

Pets come to most of us in a variety of unexpected ways. The kids come home from college with a four-legged roommate. Junior is transferred out of town and can't take his pet with him. You open a newspaper one day and there's a picture of your next four-legged family member staring right at you from the Humane Society's "Pet of the Week" column. A particular stray follows you home, and you haven't the heart to turn it away.

Thousands of pets are chosen by cold, calculated, rational reasoning, but millions more have joined our households by their own design. In the past ten years, I think I have heard most of the stories. Judging by the results, I'd have to admit that these millions of dogs, cats, and assorted other animals have done very well for themselves, and as well for their masters.

Considering the ability of some dogs and cats to travel thousands of miles to find their old masters, I can't imagine why so many animals appear at a "stranger's" doorstep, unless they were deliberately seeking a particular home. It's the most commonly told story I have heard. A family member got the urge to go to the all-night food store for cigarettes and there was this poor little ol' dog just sitting there waiting for him. Or some feline just followed the husband into the house of cat haters when he went for the Sunday paper. That was eight years ago. After all, what are you going to do with a lonely dog you find at the local Seven-Eleven or a cat that just walked in? Sometimes these guests are destined to spend the rest of their lives with their chosen family, but sometimes their visits are brief.

During the four years that Peggy and I operated a small pet motel in Florida, we had a huge ceramic flower pot containing aloe plants on each side of the entrance door. One day, we came in to find one of the plants shredded on the ground. In its place was a nesting wild mallard hen. With thousands of acres of marshland nearby, this duck decided to camp with us. Each day for thirteen days, the duck added one egg to her nest, and twenty-eight days later, they began hatching. Of course we provided her with ground corn and water, which she accepted as if due her. When the ducklings matured, she led them to our nearby lake, and then one day, they were gone. Each year she reappeared, removed our new aloe plant, and again began laying eggs. Oddly, although hundreds of hunting dogs went in and out of our doors, not one made an attempt to go after the duck. The dogs would stop and stare at the duck and she would stare back, but it was as if they had some mutual agreement to respect each other while on our grounds.

Another pair of visitors who chose us was a hen and rooster, but at least the hen paid for their corn by providing us with a nice fresh egg each day.

And let's not forget the pets that arrive as gifts. There appears to be no limit to these, as Peggy and I found out when we went into the kennel one Christmas morning and found a cute baby pig all decked out in bright red, white, and blue ribbons. Chrisy was a gift from

Kim and Cindy, two of our thoughtful employees. Chrisy enjoyed kennel life and provided a ready solution to the problem of leftover dog and cat food. She ate everything. One of her favorite pastimes was her weekly medicated bath, after which she would go directly outside and wallow in the dirt. Chrisy may have thought she was a dog, but her natural instincts could not be suppressed, and after routing up an acre of good lawn and chewing up all our external hose lines, we thought she might be more at home on our neighbor's farm.

Fox Fehling seemed destined to meet one of her pets, a Norwegian blue shadow fox. Ms. Fehling is a violinist with the Chicago Symphony Orchestra and frequently has to travel. While in Idaho, she heard of a furrier who was offering a six-week-old Norwegian fox cub for sale. Considering the possible alternative of leaving the fox with the furrier, she rushed down and purchased the cub. Today, the fox lives with Ms. Fehling, her four cats, and her dog. None of the animals are caged, and they all get along just fine.

Another of my customers told me how much she had hated cats when she was younger. Then, one day, when she opened her front door to let in her miniature schnauzer, the dog was carrying a tiny bundle of fur in its mouth. Thinking it was a dead rat, she screamed for her husband.

What appeared to be a rat turned out to be a kitten only a few days old. That was twenty-two years ago. The cat has outlived its canine mentor and his owner wouldn't trade him for a million dollars.

They are very smart, these animals, and in most cases, don't you believe they are not discriminating. They simply have a different value system! The odds that you will really choose your own pet is probably a million to one, so why worry about it. Make up your mind that at the right time and place, your four-legged prince will find you.

There are many matches that I'm sure had to be inspired. I recall a very attractive lady who used to bring her boss's dog in for boarding. Contrary to the dress conventions of the time or the nature of the weather, this young lady always wore pant suits or slacks.

One day, I arrived in the parking lot at the same time she did, and I watched her walk to the lobby with a perceptible limp. Her slacks concealed a defective limb.

She arrived at the pet motel one time to board her own dog, a small fox terrier that she had recently acquired from the Humane Society. The dog was normal in every respect except that one of its legs was atrophied. The dog walked, ran, and jumped as normally as any other dog, but with three legs instead of four.

When one of the attendants throughtlessly mentioned the handicap, the lady responded sharply, "Hey, he doesn't know he's handicapped, so don't tell him he is." She picked the dog up, hugged it, and then set it back down on the floor. "He gets around just fine," she said. And he did. They both did.

Renee Alper admits her dog chose her. Renee, a victim of psoriatic arthritis, could only get around in a wheelchair maneuvered by her constant companion, Joanne. In June 1984, Renee, looking for a dog that might help brighten her long hours of confinement, visited the Save-A-Pet Animal Foundation's kennel. Renee was wheeled from one pen to another. With so many dogs to choose from, she couldn't make up her mind, until, in one of the rooms, a small mixed terrier forced his way to the foot of her wheelchair and began licking her toes. The decision was made right then. Dumpling, an abandoned nine-month-old mixed terrier, had found a home with one fell lick.

About a year after adopting Dumpling, Renee heard about an organization called Support Dogs for the Handicapped. This organization, operating on the same principle as the Leader Dogs for the Blind Association, counseled Renee that only a special dog could be trained to perform the many tasks a Support Dog was required to do. Renee was not convinced. Instead, she had a friend make the required special harness and began teaching Dumpling to "heel" to her wheelchair. With a minimum of training, Dumpling responded and for the first time since her confinement,

Renee dared to begin taking trips out of doors without Joanne. Learning to fetch and retrieve necessary objects came easily to Dumpling and within a short time, the dog learned to answer Renee's special speaker telephone by using her mouth to lift the receiver off the cradle. The dog's ability to respond to each new challenge was uncanny. Before long, Joanne was able to move into her own bedroom, where the dog would summon her if Renee needed assistance. Both women gained a new measure of privacy and confidence. In February 1985, this hitherto unwanted mutt became the fifth dog in Illinois to be certified as an official Support Dog for the Handicapped. To many, it seems that Dumpling was saved for a special purpose and that it was more than coincidence that brought Renee to Save-A-Pet that particular day.

Another match that I suspect had to be preordained happened to two very close friends of mine, Harold and Birdie Diebert. Birdie is the kind of person who always has to have a dog in her home. Although Harold is now retired, Birdie probably spends more money on donations to various animal shelters now than she did when Harold was working at General Motors. Birdie likes to joke that Harold's pension money buys the food for their table. Her Social Security check buys the food for the local animal shelters.

In addition, every year she fills a huge basket with pet food and treats and delivers it to the local animal shelter on the day before Christmas. It's a nice custom more and more people are adopting.

Last Christmas was the only time Birdie ever missed her annual visit, and I think I know why. She had begun talking about acquiring another dog as soon as it became apparent their old dog would not live much longer. However, since they spend about six months each year traveling around the country in their motor home, Harold was not enthusiastic about getting another pet. Finally he laid down the law: No more pets.

At about this time, Birdie began to notice the German shepherd in the yard behind hers. The dog was often tied to a tree in the yard for hours on end without food or water and seemed to receive minimal attention from its owners. When Birdie checked from her kitchen window, she usually found the dog lying as close to her property line as its tether would permit, staring back at her. She got into a routine of carrying water and food to the dog whenever it appeared to have none. She even gave the dog a nickname, Jo Jo.

When their old dog passed away, Birdie decided to spare herself the pain of visiting the animal shelter that Christmas, and, instead, mailed them a cash donation. Harold didn't object to supporting another animal shelter, but he remained firm about not getting another dog.

A few days after Christmas, while doing her shopping, Birdie found herself filling her grocery cart with pet foods and all the assorted cookies and treats that people lavish on their pets. The animal shelter was about to receive a belated Christmas gift. On this occasion, perhaps as a penance, Birdie cajoled Harold into driving her there.

As she went from cage to cage, she suddenly stopped in front of one that held a large German shepherd. She stared into the dog's eyes and began shouting for Harold to come and look at it.

"Isn't that Jo Jo?" Birdie asked.

Harold laughed at the suggestion. Even the possibility was too remote.

"It is too Jo Jo," Birdie replied, continuing to study the animal.

A check with the manager confirmed that the dog was indeed the same one that had been living in the house behind theirs.

"I want him!" Birdie snapped without even looking at Harold.

"He's not a good dog," the shelter's manager warned her.

"*I want him!*" Birdie demanded with more conviction than before. Harold shook his head but never said a word.

If Birdie had visited the shelter on December 24, the day she usually made her Christmas visit, she would have missed Jo Jo because he hadn't been brought in yet. If she had visited the shelter one day later, she would have missed Jo Jo because he was due to be put to sleep.

From the day they took him home, Jo Jo became Harold's dog. You will not find one without the other. He is still unfriendly toward strangers, but he has never been anything but meek and unswervingly loyal to his new owners.

One of the interesting things about the story is that even though Jo Jo is allowed out in their unfenced yard several times a day, he has never once left their yard or even approached his former home. As they've traveled around the country in their mobile home, not once has Jo Jo ever strayed more than a few feet from his new owners' sides. I think Jo Jo picked good owners; the Dieberts actually think they picked the dog.

# 20

# A DREAM IS
# SHATTERED

From the day we opened, our concept of pet care became the benchmark of pet boarding not only in America, but throughout the world. Our uniqueness would be featured in almost every major American periodical including *Newsweek* and *U.S. News & World Report,* and we would even make the cover of *Time.*

In France, it was *Paris Match* and in Germany, *Stern.* The Japanese government sent a film crew to incorporate us into a documentary entitled "Animals and Man." In many countries of the world, a new level of pet-boarding concern gave pet owners new hope.

From *Country Gentleman* to *Penthouse* and *Mad Magazine,* regardless of a person's choice of reading, the story of a new dimension in pet care was brought to the public's attention. In the book *Amazing America,* American Pet Motels would be singled out as one of the places visitors should see if they visit the state of Illinois.

Many people learned about us from television. In addition to special news features shown on all of the major networks, our story would be included on such leading TV shows as "Real People," "Sorting It Out," "Hour Magazine," "Good Morning, America," and "P.M. Magazine," just to mention a few. Camera crews from "National Geographic" and "Ripley's Believe It or Not" also filmed our operations. Good pet care was now believable. The nicest thing was that all of this was accomplished through the word of satisfied customers, not by any efforts of an advertising agency or public relations firm.

During 1976, every room in the pet motel was booked, and at times we carried over four hundred names on a waiting list. We had to turn down even steady clients who failed to make their reservations one or two months in advance.

There was no question about our viability. It was time to begin planning our expansion.

Marketing projections were completed, identifying suitable markets for 103 new pet motels. A five-year plan was prepared calling for the addition of two more pet motels in the Chicago area and another seven in nearby metropolitan areas.

Based on revenue figures through November, we could project a gross income of almost $400,000 and a healthy after-tax profit. A second pet motel in the Chicago area would add another $50,000 to our profit just by sharing the Yellow Pages advertising costs and corporate overhead. Moreover, we had learned many lessons from our first effort. These mistakes would not be repeated, and we could expect additional profits from these economies.

Christmas of 1976 was shaping up to be the most joyous occasion of my life, and I planned it accordingly. Marc was still serving in Korea, but I notified Leslie and her husband, Michael, that I was sending them plane fare and expected them to join Gail, Peggy, and me for a festive Christmas celebration.

One thing Peggy does very well is spend money. She loves to shop, and the fact that she is buying things for someone else never diminishes her enthusiasm. For a change, I encouraged her. We were finally on our way.

Only days into December, fate, in the form of a telephone call, was to decree that such dreams were not to be. On December 5, while tending the reception counter, I received a personal call.

"Merry Christmas. American Pet Motels," I answered merrily.

There was a slight pause before the other party found his voice. It was one of Ray Kroc's lawyers. "Bob, I wanted to let you know that Ray has decided to close the pet motel on December thirty-first. He wants you out of there not later than that date.''

His words sent a cold, sobering chill through me. I was speechless as I tried to understand what was happening. The lawyer's voice broke the silence.

"We'd like you to wrap up all of your personal affairs and be off the premises as soon as possible, but in no event later than the thirty-first."

By this time I was able to catch my breath. "But, why? We're making more money than we even anticipated. We're booked full till next year. Everything points to a huge success. Why would Ray want to close the business down? Besides, we're committed to boarding almost four hundred animals until the tenth of January. What am I supposed to do, put them out on the street?"

Suddenly, a familiar voice came sharply across the telephone line. It was another of Ray's attorneys. "Don't you worry about that! We're taking care of everything!" His voice was cold and hostile.

I could not comprehend what it all really meant. Except for my opposition to the imposition of the rent and interest, I could think of nothing that might have provoked this situation. I had given in on everything they demanded. Perhaps I had given in too much, I thought. Perhaps, too easily. I searched my mind for the answer to what was happening, but the first attorney's voice brought me back to the present.

"Bob, don't worry about the business. Just be sure that you are off the premises by the thirty-first. Someone else is coming in to run the business on that date."

Suddenly there was another dimension to the matter. I had a five-year management contract. Kroc couldn't bring in someone else. "I thought you said Ray was closing the pet motel," I said.

"He is," the attorney replied. "He is dissolving the company and selling the assets to another party who intends to operate a kennel there."

"Is the new owner going to change the name of the company?" I asked.

There was a pause. "No."

"Well, if the company is being dissolved, are we going to disconnect the telephone service?"

Again the lawyer answered, "No."

It was obvious that the business was not being closed. Something else was happening.

Finally, the lawyer admitted part of the truth. "Actually, we have a buyer for the pet motel, and he has some plans to make it more profitable."

"Wait a minute," I said. "I've got a five-year contract with Ray. This is my business. It's my concept and my name. If you're going to dissolve the business, then let's dissolve it. We'll shut off the telephone and lock the doors!"

Almost immediately, the other lawyer's voice came screaming across the line. "It's not your concept or your business! It's Kroc's! It's all Kroc's!" He almost shrieked the words.

The first lawyer came back on the line. His voice was quiet and almost sympathetic. "Bob, the company does not have enough assets to satisfy Ray's claims. He is calling his notes for the one-hundred-eighty-thousand dollars for back rent and interest. Ray holds eighty-five percent of the stock and that's enough to dissolve the corporation. If you'll look at your employment contract and other agreements, you'll find that they are all with American Pet Motels. When the company is dissolved, all your contracts are voided."

I couldn't recall my attorney mentioning this aspect of the agreement to me. It was a bad time for me to receive a lesson in contract law, but I had no reason to doubt what Kroc's lawyer was saying. I had been giving Ray $60,000 a year plus 85 percent of the profit. Apparently, it still wasn't enough for the $685 million man who controlled the McDonald's empire.

"What am I going to end up with out of this?" I asked.

"Nothing. Everything belongs to Ray."

I went into shock. No matter what may have transpired, my interest in American Pet Motels had to be worth something. Certainly the name and goodwill were rightfully mine. Except for a small loss our first year, we were earning a larger, albeit still modest, profit each year. Even with the addition of the rent payment, American Pet Motels would never suffer an operating loss again. There was no way I would willingly just turn this package over to someone else.

"Look," I said. "I think that if Ray wants to close the business, we should do just that. I don't think a new buyer or anyone else should be entitled to maintain continuity of operation by stepping in here and milking the name and goodwill of American Pet Motels."

My words must have struck a nerve. Once again the hostile voice came back on the line. "Listen! It doesn't matter what you think! You don't own anything. In fact, you owe Ray Kroc money. You've got nothing coming and we want you out of there."

The other lawyer interrupted. "Bob, with the purchase of the San Diego Padres and his other investments, Ray has had an unusual amount of income this year which needs sheltering. We've no other choice but to sell American Pet Motels and use the loss to offset some of Ray's income."

The frivolousness and shallow logic offered stunned me. There was nothing more I could think of to say. Instead, I just muttered, "O.K." and hung up. Turning, I saw my bookkeeper and the receptionist looking at me.

"Kroc is closing down the pet motel on December thirty-first," I said.

Suddenly, tears began to well up in my eyes. I held my head down against my chest and blindly made my way back to the seclusion of my office. For the first time, the full implications of what was going to happen struck me. I sat down at my desk and buried my head in my arms and began to cry. I could not restrain myself any longer.

"Oh, God," I asked, "what have I done to deserve this? What did I ever do to this man? To anyone? With all of his millions. With all of his wealth, why would he do this? How could a man like him do this?"

For the balance of the day, I remained there. I could not stem the flow of tears, and my throat ached from trying. A sharp, tearing pain caused an almost unbearable cramp in my chest. I simply could not understand how this could really happen in view of everything Ray and Joan Kroc had said.

Intermittently, I recalled my conversations with them. "Don't worry about a thing." "We're doing this all for you." "We don't care if the business never makes a dime." "We have more wealth than we'll ever need. We just want to see you and Peggy become wealthy and enjoy some of the luxuries we do."

Over and over again, I kept recalling their glowing assurances of trust and confidence. The popular McDonald's jingle came into my mind. "We do it all for you."

"Yes, you certainly do," I thought. "You'll do it to anyone!"

Driving home that night, I began to realize what I was up against. Except for a few thousand dollars in mutual funds and General Motors stock, I had completely exhausted our savings. Bolstered by the assurances that I would never have anything to worry about again, I had not made any effort to rebuild our depleted finances.

To make the company look better and improve our profitability during the start-up period, I had personally absorbed as many trivial expenses as my salary permitted. When I took guests and business associates out for lunch or dinner, I paid the expenses from my personal account. Even the company's typewriter and calculator, as well as most of the office supplies, I had furnished in the naive belief that all of this was an investment that I would recoup with our future success.

Not only had I not taken the minimum precautions to protect Peggy and the children against such a catastrophe, I had even encouraged them to believe that our mode of living was just the minimum of what they might expect. I began counting up the numerous monthly obligations we had acquired with our benign sense of security. They were overwhelming.

I was almost fifty years old. How long would it take before I would find suitable employment? How would we live? How would we face our friends and neighbors? But, above all, what would they turn American Pet Motels into once I was out of the way?

In a brief instant, I had plunged from the pinnacle of success to the very nadir of failure. I had gambled everything we had and lost. Our pension program, our stock savings program, all was gone. Worse, I had talked Peggy into letting me sell her dream home and invest the money in my pet motel fantasy. My promise to replace it one day seemed remote now.

It was all one gigantic deception. I had cheated her not only out of what she already had, but of any future well-being as well.

All of my life I had lived a fairy tale, believing that honest endeavor and hard work would bring us happiness and success. That naive Irish father of mine was wrong. Horribly wrong.

How ironic that Kroc, who had traveled a similar path to mine, would be the one to destroy this myth. He could buy his respect in the marketplace of public opinion. Price is no object for a man who has $685 million. His $3 million donation to the local zoo for an ape house would buy him more honors than any breach of integrity could ever tarnish.

The pain of insecurity sharpened as I opened the front door to our house. Casanova and Koira came bounding down the stairs to greet me, but I had no treats to offer them this time. It was a ritual I never tired of, but this day I had no stomach for it. I pushed past the dogs and walked toward the bedroom.

It is strange what irrational and seemingly insignificant thoughts you think at a time like this. I was wondering where we would get money to buy them dog food and to get them groomed. What would happen if we were forced to live where they would not permit pets? What would happen to my dogs?

These seemingly trivial matters became of paramount importance to me and served to reinforce the terrible burden that weighed on my mind.

I closed the bedroom door behind me and locked it. My eyes were blurred with yet more tears as I considered the dimensions of my failure. I opened the bottom door of the night stand and reached behind the heating pad for the .38 caliber service revolver I kept there.

Life was too full of disappointment to want to experience any more. I wanted it to end. I wanted it to end now.

# 21

# THE DECISION
# IS MADE

There had been a time when I believed suicide was a worthless and futile gesture, meaningless and unsupportive. No longer.

I had known several persons, some close friends, who had committed suicide. My very best friend deliberately drank himself to death, while another friend, with whom I had shared numerous harrowing wartime experiences, literally starved himself to death. The beautiful wife of a well-known radio personality talked to Peggy about going shopping and that afternoon took her life with an overdose of sleeping pills.

Each time, I shook my head and lamented the useless and tragic waste of life. Now, for the first time, I could understand and share their compulsion to flee this life—a life where dreams and aspirations are suddenly snatched away, where a tranquil existence is suddenly replaced by hopeless despair, where one's absolute faith is betrayed by someone he most trusts.

Suicide is not an act that I would ever condone or even justify for another. But, for me, this was the point beyond which continued existence became too bitter to sustain.

I consider myself an extremely religious person, although I attend no church on a regular basis and do not surround myself with religion's visible trappings. I had moved through these experiences in my youth. Over the years, I had formulated a dogma that I subscribed to with the reverence of the most venerable deist. I had come to accept that the magnitude of order in the universe makes it impossible to deny the existence of some supreme power. But, my conception of this deity differed from most traditionalists. My God was an understanding and forgiving God. He created me in His image, and to a lesser degree endowed me with all His powers. Even the greatest powers, to create life and to take it, were mine.

I believed that it was not without purpose that He had put me here on earth, but that although this purpose may not be revealed to me, the least He expected was that I live my life so no man could claim an injury or harm of my deliberate doing.

Beyond this, my God expected little more of me. Not being a pompous or vain God, I knew that He would understand this one last act of contrition.

I opened the chamber of the revolver and turned the cylinder slowly around until a filled chamber was opposite the barrel, and then I locked the cylinder in place.

No one had loved or appreciated life with a fervor greater than I. Now, lying across the bed with the cocked revolver in my hand, I suddenly began recalling how many times I had been at the brink of death, only to be led back to safety by some unseen hand of fate.

I thought about the time when, as a sixteen-year-old member of a flying circus, I had fallen ten thousand feet with both of my parachutes fouled, and survived. During World War II, I had served in the South Pacific with the Maritime Service until I was old enough to become an air cadet in the American Air Force. I was the only air cadet to go through basic training with more theater ribbons than most of my instructors. I was one of ten people who walked away from the crash of a Lockheed Constellation in Zetek, Czechoslovakia. At twenty-one, I trained and commanded the first Israeli Airborne Brigade during the Middle East War. By my twenty-second birthday, I had made over 160 parachute jumps, and had been involved in three wars, suffering little more than a concussion.

There were so many times, so many close calls. I opened my eyes to the stark reality of the room around me. The handle of my revolver seemed strangely cold and unfriendly.

"Good God!" I remarked under my breath. "Is this how it's all going to end?"

Suddenly, the room around me seemed to fill with a dustlike cloud. I saw cattle, thousands of cattle being driven by hooping and hollering cowboys. I could actually smell the dust and hear their raucous voices. Like a version of an old John Wayne movie, I saw the stereotyped villain counting his money and telling his hired hands that the range land was his. All his. He would drive the homesteaders off the range and it would be all his.

I knew it wouldn't happen this way. In every Western movie that I had ever seen, the homesteaders finally stood up and fought back against the overwhelming odds, to win in the end.

"Is this so different?" I asked myself.

I had been so close to death so many times, and yet each time fate had snatched me back and permitted me to continue living. The right to honest endeavor and to the fruits of that labor was my sacred heritage.

If my ancestors had the guts to stand up to the beef barons of yesterday, the least I could do was to stand up to the ground-beef barons of today.

There had to be a purpose to my life.

In that instant, I knew I mustn't give up. I had no idea how, but I would fight Ray Kroc and his $685 million if it was the last thing I did. I placed the revolver back in the night stand and fell into a deep sleep.

Saturday morning, I drove into work confident that a phone call to an attorney would bring salvation. I was emotionally exhausted, but the simple belief that Kroc's actions were contrary to every part of our agreement gave me the confidence necessary to try and save what I felt was really mine.

I sat down and, beginning with the As, began calling law firms listed in the Yellow Pages. I selected those firms where a string of names appeared in their listing, hoping it might imply a higher degree of effectiveness by virtue of numbers.

My first problem was that many firms were closed on

Saturday. My second problem was more serious. Most of the lawyers I did speak to were of a common mind. As soon as I mentioned the name of Ray Kroc and my limited financial resources, the discussion came to an abrupt end. One law firm after another confirmed that Kroc's 85 percent equity gave him the right to do anything he wanted with the corporation. The process of proving he had broken specific agreements could involve thousands and thousands of dollars and years of litigation. Without the financial resources to match Kroc's millions, one attorney after another counseled me to walk away and save what I had.

It was afternoon before I reached the Ws and the name Walsh, Case and Coale. Robert O. Case, a senior partner, patiently listened to my story. I could sense his reluctance, but I pleaded for his assistance. Finally, he agreed to meet with me on Sunday and study the merits of the case.

It was Sunday, December 7, Pearl Harbor Day.

Case arrived on time and brought with him Ralph Brown, the firm's senior trial lawyer. They listened as I told them the entire story. They conceded that all of the written documents appeared to favor Kroc's position. "However," they added, "his motion of dissolving the company and then immediately reopening it with the same name, telephone numbers, and mode of operation suggests his actions are just a ploy to deprive the minority stockholder of his equity."

While I didn't want to admit it, the possibility that the entire business arrangement was set up from the very beginning with this in mind became a very real consideration.

After lengthy consideration, the two lawyers came up with a proposal. Their firm would take my case on the basis that, if we lost, I would only pay them their actual labor costs and out-of-pocket expenses. If we won, I would pay them their regular fee, which could amount to many thousands of dollars. I accepted.

There was one other requirement. An $8,500 retainer had to be paid before they would begin their efforts. With only a fraction of that available, I nonetheless shook hands on the agreement.

The prospect of winning was dampened considerably

when the lawyers advised me that even if I won, there could be no punitive damage award. The most I could expect out of a lawsuit was to force Kroc into continuing the company's existence. There would remain a variety of options for him to exercise his wrath once my employment agreement expired.

That night, I explained our options to Peggy. For a person who feared the unknown and was almost paranoid about financial security, her prompt response surprised me. "Let's fight them no matter what it costs!"

A check for $4,000 was put in the mail that evening. The balance of the retainer was paid over the next few weeks as the money from the sale of our stocks and mutual funds dribbled in. The mortgage company approved a second mortgage on my house, but beyond that and what I had in hand, I had no idea of how I would pay any additional legal fees. I was gambling everything we had on our judicial system. I did not consider losing. I could not even conceive of what was happening being adjudged as legal.

During the next two weeks, I had only two messages from McDonald's. One was a warning that if I didn't just walk away, Ray's lawyers would look up every bar I ever got drunk in, every girl I ever slept with, and would ruin me socially, politically, and economically, if it took $685 million to do it. That was one of the many times I have reflected back over my life and not regretted living a comparatively virtuous existence. In response, I offered them my war record.

The second item was a solitary envelope bearing McDonald's return address. It contained a single sheet of paper, a Xeroxed cartoon. It was a picture of the earth with people standing on it elbow to elbow. From out of the clouds above was coming a booming voice, and the caption beneath the cartoon read, "Listen to Me Earthlings. This Is God! I'm Repossessing Earth and I Want Everyone Off by the 31st!" Although several McDonald's executives still board their pets with me, no one has ever mentioned the cartoon, let alone admitted to sending it.

Shortly before the end of the month, a special messenger carried a legal brief to the offices of Kroc's attorneys. It contained a copy of the documents in which I was charging the founder and chairman of the board of McDonald's Corporation with stock fraud. The suit was being filed in a federal court.

America's ground-beef baron would have to face a homesteader at the bar of justice.

# 22

# AGAIN . . . AGAIN . . . AND AGAIN

The suit did not go to court.

After three and a half months of negotiations, an out-of-court agreement was reached. I would buy the Krocs' interest in American Pet Motels by paying $5,000 a month plus 15 percent of the profits for ten years. At the end of the ten years, I would have to make a balloon payment of another $650,000.

It was a horrendous price, but what price is too high to sustain a dream? Ten years would give me time to obtain a conventional mortgage and time in which to build the other two pet motels west and south of Chicago. In ten years, a lot could happen, and it did.

It seemed as if even the gods had conspired against us. The oil embargo of the late seventies and the subsequent skyrocketing price of gasoline created havoc with the travel industry. People stopped traveling. No longer did they board the family pet and take off on their extended vacations. Weekend trips to neighboring states became an unnecessary luxury, and our waiting list for rooms seemed to disappear overnight.

Yet while airlines, hotels, and other leisure-time industries were going belly up in one of the worst recessions to hit the travel industry, we continued to make a slight profit without cutting our services. Ten years, however, was not enough time to destroy the image that a kennel was a ma and pa operation. Even though bankers had pets of their own and were aware of the problems that wracked the boarding industry, they remained as unconvinced that any substantial effort to improve it justified the risk of a loan, as when I started nineteen years before. Skyrocketing interest rates and a scarcity of money diminished the prospects of resolving our dilemma. As 1985 approached, the probability of refinancing our note to the Krocs seemed hopeless, and we began preparing to close the business.

Peggy and I sold our home in Chicago's suburbs and purchased a small kennel in Sarasota, Florida. The transaction was handled in such a way that the property couldn't be touched if the Krocs forced us into bankruptcy. Marc took over the operation of American Pet Motels and was to run it until it closed. It was a depressing time, but despite the gloomy outlook, we still refused to give up. Instead, we redoubled our efforts to obtain new financing to pay off the note.

Perseverance would be rewarded. But it was not until December 1984, only a few months before our note came due, that a sympathetic savings and loan association in Lyons, Illinois, agreed to lend us a half million dollars providing we could raise the additional $150,000 from someone else.

The balance of the money we needed came from an unexpected source, Joan Kroc. Although Ray Kroc had steadfastly refused to alter the terms of the note up until his death in 1984, his wife, Joan, did not remain indifferent to our problem. To save us from defaulting, Mrs. Kroc discounted the old note $50,000 and agreed to carry the $100,000 balance for five more years at only 14 percent interest.

Final resolution of the note was like getting a new lease on life. Not a reprieve, but a vindication of all the past optimism, efforts, and sacrifices.

When all of the loan documents had been signed and the immediate future of American Pet Motels reasonably secured, I remarked to Peggy that we had now reached a new financial milestone in our lives. We had achieved the dubious distinction of having mortgage payments of over $11,000 a month. Peggy's response amused me more than it reassured me. She reminded me of a time not too far in the past when a finance company turned us down for a loan to purchase a used Kaiser automobile because they didn't feel we could make the monthly payments of thirty-nine dollars. We had come a long way.

The realization of being able to continue in our quest again spawned the dream of building more pet motels throughout America, but we realized this could best be done living in Chicago. With some reluctance, we sold the kennel in Florida and loaded our three dogs and our belongings into our van and headed back home.

Sometimes, events tempt you to ask yourself just how far you really have come. This question arises in my mind each time an old friend asks us if we would do it all over again.

"Knowing what you were giving up and all the problems you would be encountering, would you do it all again? Was it worth it?"

I might pause, but my answer will always be the same. If there were ten years of sleepless nights, there were ten years of days filled with love and satisfaction beyond the comprehension of those who have never worked with animals.

It is said that some people march to a different drummer. Mine has been a symphony. A rhapsody of creature sounds filled with a quality of love and affection that is almost alien to the society we live in.

The dream of improving the quality of pet care in America was not a fantasy. It was and remains a viable goal. From the time we purchased Kroc's interest in American Pet Motels in order to preserve its integrity, until the day we signed the mortgage that lifted the uncertainty of our future, I never went to sleep without asking myself if it was worth it. Over and over during those nine long years, I would awaken in the middle of the night and ask myself if it had all been a dream or a nightmare. A quest of love or an obsession born of frustration? How cruel the prison of our aspirations can be. But what an education it has been. For us, as well as for thousands of pet owners and people in our industry. We learned that commercial boarding facilities *can* be designed, built, and managed to preclude the tragic consequences many pet owners experienced. Kennels *can* be clean and odorless. You *can* employ workers who are mature and caring and have a management that is concerned. *Any* pet can be boarded with the expectation that it will be alive and healthy when it goes home. Pet owners *do* have a choice.

Coming in contact with many thousands of pet owners has awakened us to the very real bond that exists between people and their pets. Pets are no longer mere chattels of the law. We acknowledge them now as "companion animals," a term that implies much, much more. It is a term that explains the people who couldn't afford shoes but who found the money to have their sick pet nursed back to health. We have grown up in a world where people have grown farther and farther apart from each other while growing closer and closer to their pets, and now we can understand why. Imagine what we would have missed.

I often think of one of my favorite boarders, a little mongrel terrier named Trouble McLain. From the day he came to us, Trouble has always refused to eat his food from such a plebeian surface as the floor. Each morning when breakfast is served, he picks his food dish up in his mouth and sets it at the end of his bed. Then, he climbs onto the bed and dines in a reclining position. Breakfast in bed. That's how it has to be for Trouble. In some parts of the world, even formal dining with one's pet is an accepted practice. In Europe, I have been in some of the finest restaurants and watched as well-dressed patrons at nearby tables fed their canine companions tidbits from their own plates.

In exchange for their unique devotion, we have pampered our creature friends without the slightest tinge of guilt. There must be a million dogs who share their master's toast each morning. There's nothing so unusual about dogs that get bacon and eggs at the pet motel. Or cats that drink chocolate milk. Or dachshunds that get a piece of beer salami at bedtime. Or horses that want to live a dog's life. If we hadn't followed our dream, we might have missed all of them. Over 100,000 dogs and cats, and thousands of other pets from a tiny mouse to a six-foot iguana. They have added a wonderful dimension to what might otherwise have been a pedestrian existence.

We would have missed meeting the hundreds of veterinarians and kennel operators who have selflessly dedicated their entire lives to the healing and welfare of our creature friends. Those whose actions embarrass these honorable professions are insignificant compared to those whose daily endeavors distinguish them.

Above all, we would have missed witnessing a lot of young men and women learning a little more about responsibility and caring through their work at the pet motel. It was an experience that we shared and profited from.

There are almost eighty-four million households in America, and three out of four include some kind of pet. Over one hundred million dogs and cats and more than seventeen million other assorted animals now share our daily living experience, and a recent survey confirmed what I've known all along: Eighty percent of all pet owners considered their pet "a member of the family."

The mystique of pet ownership defies any simple logic. It is universal and all-pervasive, but only lately are serious attempts being made to determine how significant a role pets play in our complex existence.

Certain benefits are already becoming clear. At a recent conference on the human/companion animal bond, the chairman reported on the startling results of a documented study of two groups of patients who had been hospitalized for heart disease. Of the patients who owned pets, only 6 percent died within one year of their hospitalization. Of those who did not own pets, 44 percent died in the same period. Who is to say that the dramatic increase in our life expectancy has not in some measure been attributable to the accompanying increase in pet ownership?

A whole body of data is now developing to suggest that both our mental and physical well-being can be significantly enhanced through ownership of a pet. For those of us who have worked with animals, nothing that will be revealed in these studies will come as a surprise. Yet despite all the benefits we derive from this association, our recognition of these benefits is oftentimes woefully inadequate. Our concern for the proper care of boarded pets is but a small effort to redress this problem.

In our society, there is a tendency for many to equate

wealth with success. If that were true, there would be many in this profession who would fail to meet the criteria. A part of our wealth is the satisfaction we get from providing the best environment a pet can have when away from its home. Sometimes this is acknowledged by the events we witness.

Last winter, a friend of mine approached her kennel one cold morning and was startled to see a large animal lying in front of the entrance, half covered by the newly fallen snow. Its gray muzzle blended into the matted snow, and its sunken eyes peered up into my friend's.

As she got closer, the old dog struggled to its feet, and its tail began a back-and-forth motion. My friend immediately recognized it as one which had been boarded frequently in recent months by an elderly woman who required intermittent hospitalization.

Upon calling the owner's home, my friend learned that the lady had died the previous day. Neither of her two married sons wanted her dog, so they had planned on having it euthanized after they finished loading their cars with their mother's "more valuable" possessions. Sometime during their goings in and out, the dog slipped out of the house and traveled over seven miles to the only other place it felt it was wanted, the kennel where it had been boarded. The dog was right. My friend found him a nice home on her father's farm.

Would we do it again knowing all the confrontations, financial sacrifices, and heartaches that lay ahead?

No degree of achievement is ever diminished by the honest effort expended. It is not the quantity of life that matters, but the quality. I had once told my son the story of how my father used to conduct the details of his painting business at an ancient roll-top desk in the basement of our old frame house in Detroit. I was only nine or ten years old, and I didn't understand the Depression years, but I loved to stand beside him and watch him do his paperwork. A single bulb hung from a strand of wire and provided the only light by which he labored. The scenario of business held a compelling fascination for me.

This one evening, my father was just sitting at the desk, not measuring the details of any blueprints or scribbling a list of figures on one of his many pads of lined paper. Even though he was owed more than enough money to pay our bills, he could not collect enough to buy groceries, let alone meet our mortgage payments. Most of the papers that now cluttered his desk were past-due bills. One conspicuous document was a notification that the bank was repossessing our home. We were hopelessly in debt, and there was no bright prospect for our future welfare. I remember my father just staring and staring at his desk top until suddenly he seemed to become aware that I was standing beside him.

He gazed down into my unenlightened face and smiled. "Just think," he said, "someday all this will be yours."

With all the ignorance youth can muster, I was enthralled at the prospect.

When Marc and I left the mortgage company with the new loan documents under my arm, Marc placed a hand on my shoulder and broke into a big grin.

"Congratulations, Dad. You now owe almost a million dollars and your monthly payments are more than you make. Do me one favor, please. Don't tell me that one day it will all be mine."

I knew Marc was joking, just as his grandfather was those many years ago. In the seven years since he joined us, Marc has shown all the signs of one hopelessly smitten by the concerns of this industry, and he eagerly anticipates the building of more pet motels. Despite the uncertainties and impositions, his dedication and effort never wavered. Peggy and I were never alone in our travail.

Would we do it all again?

The good Lord willing, again . . . and again . . . and again. . . .

# APPENDIX

## SELECTING A BOARDING FACILITY

How do you choose the proper pet-boarding facility?

The pet owner should be aware that "big" is not necessarily "better," any more than a good appearance can be the single criterion for good care. There are a number of factors for the concerned pet owner to consider when he makes his selection, and many of these will be found listed at the end of this section.

Recognizing the public's need for a comprehensive list of pet-boarding facilities, several pet-food manufacturers and trade associations now offer such a list for sale. Unfortunately, these lists of "good kennels" include only kennels who purchase the pet-food manufacturers' particular brand of dog food or only those kennels who belong to that particular trade organization. To be included, a kennel is not required to be air-conditioned or heated or to provide any minimal degree of proper care.

Nor are fancy plaques, awards, or membership displays necessarily indicative of good care. The largest trade association, the American Boarding Kennels Association, will accept almost any kennel for membership as long as their dues are kept current. Despite the cruel and disreputable practices prevalent in this industry, very few local municipalities or states have laws requiring the inspection and licensing of pet-boarding facilities. Illinois, one of the exceptions, requires licensing and regular inspections by the Department of

Agriculture, which closes between thirty and forty kennels a year (including one recently that made a practice of burying dogs alive). The American Boarding Kennels Association publicly opposes the inspection or licensing of kennels by any legal body. In fact, their code of ethics includes the provision that it is unethical for any member to slander or defame the actions or business practices of the boarding industry. While a member, the author became the first brought up on charges of being "unethical," for publishing a statement that the boarding industry was one of the most unethical, unprofessional, and unscrupulous industries in America.

Fortunately for pet owners, a new association of pet-boarding operators, the Societé pour la Promotion et le Developement des Chenils (Society for the Advancement of Pet Boarding Care), is now being formed. In addition to lobbying for city and state regulations to improve conditions, membership requires strict compliance with a rigid code of ethics. A kennel can only receive the society's seal of approval by meeting a comprehensive list of requirements.

As a minimum, when seeking a pet-boarding facility, pet owners would be wise to follow the society's "Ten Commandments of Pet Boarding."

### Ten Commandments of Pet Boarding

1. **THOU SHALT NOT** board in any facility that will not let you see where your pet will be kept.
2. **THOU SHALT NOT** board in any facility that boards sick animals in the same general area as are kept boarded pets.
3. **THOU SHALT NOT** board in any facility that is not clean and well kept inside and outside.
4. **THOU SHALT NOT** board in any facility that does not require proof of vaccinations.
5. **THOU SHALT NOT** board in any facility that employs immature or incompetent employees to clean or care for the animals.
6. **THOU SHALT NOT** board your dog in a cage or pen unless you know it will receive three twenty-minute exercise periods daily, regardless of the weather.

7. **THOU SHALT NOT** board your pet in a facility that lacks properly designed ventilation to maintain the ambient temperature between 55 and 85 degrees Fahrenheit for all warm-blooded animals.
8. **THOU SHALT NOT** board your pet in a facility that will not contact your own veterinarian in event of a serious illness or injury.
9. **THOU SHALT NOT** board your pet in a facility that does not feed the animals and clean and disinfect their accommodations as required and never less than once in every 24-hour period.
10. **THOU SHALT NOT** board your pet in a facility that permits the boarding of different owners' pets in the same space.

These ten commandments are the least a pet owner should demand from a kennel.

There are numerous other factors that one should consider. The following is a comprehensive list contained in a brochure distributed by the American Pet Motels. Some of the items are also covered by the "Ten Commandments of Pet Boarding."

### 41 Ways to Choose a Kennel or Cattery General

*General*

1. Are you permitted to inspect the facilities?
2. Is the general appearance of the facilities favorable?
3. Is there protection in the event of fire? (Is the facility fire resistant? Is it sprinklered? Is there fire-fighting equipment on the premises?)
4. Have the employees been trained how to save the animals in the event of a fire or natural disaster?
5. Are trained animal attendants available to take care of the animals seven days a week, including Sundays and holidays?
6. Does the kennel offer a written boarding agreement in which they accept liability for the loss of your pet due to escape, injury, illness, or death due to their negligence?
7. Is the use of tranquilizers strictly forbidden?

**187**

8. Is emergency veterinary service available twenty-four hours a day?
9. Does the management require written evidence of a pet's immunization against rabies and distemper?
10. Do they prohibit bringing sick animals on the premises for treatment?
11. Are there an adequate number of trained personnel to care for all the pets?
12. Are service charges reasonable?

## Cleanliness

13. Are the animal facilities sanitized not less than once a day with an acknowledged disinfectant that is harmless?
14. Do the employees appear neat and clean?
15. Are the grounds kept clean and free of animal waste and debris?
16. Are the grounds treated to minimize flies, mosquitoes, ticks, and other harmful insects?
17. In areas of heavy flea and/or tick populations, are all incoming pets checked for infestation?

## Animal Facilities

18. Does the facility prohibit the use of wood facilities for the boarding of all house pets?
19. Do dogs and cats have off-the-floor sleeping facilities?
20. Do animal runs have sealed concrete or plastic floors instead of gravel, dirt, or wood?
21. Does each dog-run divider include a twenty-four-inch-high solid urine barrier?
22. Does every dog and cat have its own private area, totally protected from the adjoining boarding areas?
23. Does every dog have an adjoining private outdoor exercise area or is it at least taken out into a clean area and exercised for twenty minutes, three times a day?
24. Is the use of "chicken" wire, wire fabric, or wire cloth prohibited for use as dog or cat enclosures?
25. Are chain link enclosures made of at least eleven-

gauge electroplated wire with a maximum mesh of not more than one and one-half inches?

26. Are the tops and bottoms of all chain link fencing knuckled (turned backward and crimped) to prevent punctures and cuts?
27. Is the use of any barbed wire on animal enclosures prohibited?
28. In addition to enclosed animal runs, is the entire kennel enclosed within a security fence?
29. Is fresh drinking water always available to the pets?
30. Are cats always boarded in a separate area than the dogs?
31. Does each cat boarding area include an exercise step?
32. Is a record maintained of each pet's eating and elimination?
32. Are feeding dishes sterilized after each use or disposable dishes used?
33. Are cat litter boxes sanitized and the litter changed daily or more often if required?

*Environment*

34. Is the heating and cooling equipment designed for, and built into, the facility?
35. Are animal quarters heated if the temperature drops to fifty-five degrees?
36. Are animal quarters air conditioned if the temperature reaches eighty-five degrees?
37. Do animal facilities receive a minimum of six fresh air changes per hour?

*Special Services*

38. Do all pets have frequent contact with humans?
39. Will the kennel provide special diets?
40. Will the kennel administer special medications?
41. Will the kennel perform reasonable special requests for your pet at a reasonable charge?

If you can answer "yes" to all these questions, you will have found a rare kennel indeed.

It is unlikely that many boarding facilities will include all of these recommendations. However, the pet owner would be well advised to seek a facility offering those features most important to their concerns.

Unfortunately, the most important consideration isn't readily observable and can't be reduced to writing. This is the integrity of the kennel operator.

A kennel that doesn't turn on its air conditioning is no better than the kennel that has none. Although the Society for the Advancement of Pet Boarding Care may be a force in the realization of improved pet care, real reform will not come about until pet owners speak out in unison and demand their concerns be addressed.

There is one other immediate way pet owners can help. Almost every town has more than one pet-boarding facility. Support the one that best meets your criteria. It's the least your pet deserves.

Mr. Leeds can be contacted by writing to him at P. O. Box 931, Wheeling, IL 60090

# INDEX

Abandoned pets, 109-13
Air system, 33, 35-36, 38
American Pet Motels
  abandoned pets, 109-13
  acclimating animals to, 89-90
  administration of
      pills/medication, 151
  air system, 33, 35-36, 38
  aquarium, 40
  aviary, 39, 98-101
  bathing/grooming salon, 40-41,
      139-43
  beginning of idea, 15-18, 25
  cattery, 36-39
  check-in procedure, 85-86
  closing by Kroc, 167-71
  construction inadequacies, 65-67,
      92-93
  construction of, 61, 63-64
  disease control, 33, 35
  dog-training classes, 101-103
  employees of, 76-83
  exotic guests, 72-74
  financing of, 42-63
  food "report card," 120-21
  grand opening of, 65-66
  "Hierarchy of Obligations," 76-77
  Imperial/Regency suites, 28-30
  indoor-outdoor runs, 32, 35
  kennel facilities, 28-36
  Kroc, Joan, 62-63, 64, 65, 179
  Kroc, Ray, 49-66, 167-71
  lawsuit/settlement, 175-78, 179-80
  lifetime boarding, 113-15
  mailboxes for pets, 30-31
  old animals, policy for, 148
  opening of, 67
  parvovirus incident, 131-38
  Pet-I-Care warranty, 123-24, 127,
      131
  publicity/coverage by media, 165
  refusal of pets, conditions for,
      67-68, 107-109
  stables, 103-105
  stress reduction, 27-28, 31
  tours of, 86
Anemia, and fleas, 144
Apes, antics of, 74-75
Appetite problems, and stress,
    121-22
Aquarium, 40

Aviary, 39, 98-101
  design of, 98-99
  talking birds, 99-100

Bathing/grooming salon, 40-41,
    139-43
Birds, aviary, 39, 98-101
Blindness, old age and, 149-50
Boarding facility, guidelines in
    choice of, 185-90
Brown, Bernie, 102-103

Canine parvovirus incident, 131-38
Cats, pregnant women and, 79-80
Cattery
  no visitors rule, 37, 38
  rhinotracheitis epidemic, 125-28
  viral infection problem, 36-37
Check-in procedure, 85-86
  acclimation of animals, 89-90
Construction, of pet motel, 61,
    63-64
Corbin, James, 37

Disease
  canine parvovirus incident,
      131-38
  rhinotracheitis epidemic, 125-28
  toxoplasmosis, 79-80
Disease control, at pet motel, 32, 35
Dogs
  canine parvovirus incident,
      131-38
  matting problem, 140-43
  most social breeds, 157
Dog training classes, 101-103
  and Bernie Brown, 102-103
Double dipping, 22, 23

Employees
  benefits to, 77
  drug searches, 79
  in-house training, 81
  pregnancy and cats, 79
  selective hiring, value of, 76
  sensitivity of, 82-83
  women verses men, 81
  wrong persons hired, case
      examples, 77-79
Escaping, animals adept at, 73-75

Euthanasia, 82–83
  court order, case example, 115–18
  motel policy, 83

Financing, 42–63
  obstacles/refusals, 43–47
  and Ray Kroc, 49–66, 94–97
Fish, aquarium, 40
Fleas
  cause of anemia, 144
  infestation of facility, 144–45

Goats, boarding of, 73, 105–106
Grooming salon, 40–41, 139–43
  and flea problem, 144–45
  and matting problem, 140–43
  for health, 139–40
  lack of, consequences, 140–41, 143
  reluctant dog, 141–43

"Hierarchy of Obligations," 76–77
Horses, boarding of, 103–105

Iguana, boarding of, 72
Imperial suite, 28–30
Injured wildlife, help to, 71–72

Kennel
  facilities, at pet motel, 28–36
  mattresses used, 35, 65
  off-hours pick up problem, 84–85
  vicious dogs, 107
Kroc, Joan, 62–63, 64, 65, 179
Kroc, Ray, 49–66
  closes pet motel, 167–71
  deceptive motive of, 175
  fiscal demands of, 94–97
  initial financing, 49–66
  lawsuit/settlement with Leeds,
    175–78, 179–80

Lifetime boarding, 113–15

Mailboxes, for pets, 30–31
Mattresses, for kennel, 35, 65
Maxwell, Gertrude, 64
Medication, giving to pets, 151
Monkeys, antics of, 74–75

Old animals
  blindness, 149–50
  policy of pet motel, 148

Pet boarding industry
  double dipping, 22, 23
  guidelines for choosing facility,
    185–90
  inadequacies of, 19
  splitting runs, 23–24

Pet-I-Care warranty, 123–24, 127
Pet motel. See American Pet Motels.
Pet owners
  acquisition of pets, 158–64
  conversations with pets, 86
  dissatisfaction/complaints of,
    152–55
  and exotic pets, 72–74
  feelings about pets, 68
  separation anxiety of, 69, 84–85,
    86, 88–89
  special instructions from, 87–88,
    90–91
  studies of, 182
  tour of pet motel, 86
Pregnant employees, danger from
  cats, 79–80

Raccoon, antics of, 73–74
Regency suite, 28–30
Reptiles
  boarding of, 39, 68–69
  feeding live animals issue, 70
Responsibilities/obligations, of pet
  motel, 76–77
Rhinotracheitis, epidemic in cattery,
  125–28
Runs, indoor-outdoor at motel, 32,
  35

Save-A-Pet Animal Foundation, 64
Separation anxiety, of pet owners,
  69, 84–85, 86, 88–89
Snakes
  boarding of, 39, 68–69
  feeding issue, 70
Special instructions, from pet
  owners, 87–88, 90–91
Splitting runs, 23–24
Stables, 103–105
Stress
  appetite problems/weight loss
    from, 121–22
  as boarding problem, 119
  reduction at pet model, 27–28, 31

Toxoplasmosis, cat and pregnant
  women, 79–80
Training, of employees, 81
Turtle, boarding of, 72–73

Veterinary community, reaction to
  pet motel, 129–30

Warranty, Pet-I-Care warranty,
  123–24, 127, 131
Weight loss, and stress, 121–22
Widmark, Patricia, 103